IT H·A·P·P·E·N·E·D IN HOCKEY

WEIRD & WONDERFUL STORIES FROM CANADA'S GREATEST GAME

BRIAN McFARLANE

Dear Brandon,

Merry Christmas!

With Much Love,

Uncle Kent, Aunt Bronwyn,

Averill and Caitlin

Stoddart

First published in 1991 by
Stoddart Publishing Co. Limited
34 Lesmill Road
Toronto, Canada
M3B 2T6

Fourth Printing September 1994

Canadian Cataloguing in Publication Data

McFarlane, Brian, 1931 –
It happened in hockey

ISBN 0-7737-5465-2

1. Hockey – Canada. I. Title.

GV848.4.C3M34 1991   796.96 '2' 0971   C91-094809-7

COVER DESIGN: Leslie Styles
COVER PHOTOGRAPH: Dan Paul
DESIGN: Brant Cowie / ArtPlus Limited

Printed in Canada

CONTENTS

Preface *vii*

PART 1 — Players

Bucko the Bodychecker *3*
How the Habs Got Beliveau *4*
Fournier the Fireman *7*
The Player Who Couldn't Score *8*
Clancy Held a Hot Hand *9*
Bill Barilko's Final Goal *11*
The Alfie Moore Saga *14*
Stardom Denied *15*
Blood in Boston *16*
Brimsek's Brilliance *17*
The Stingiest Goalie *18*
"Sudden Death" Hill *19*
Cool Head, Nervous Stomach *20*
A Fast Start *22*
Sawchuk's Dazzling Playoffs *24*
Battle of the Bulge *25*
One of Hockey's Oldest Records *27*
A Million for Mahovlich *27*
Oh, Brother *28*
Baun Scores the Winner — On a Broken Leg *29*
An Unbeatable Goaltending Streak *30*
Goalies Are Different *31*
Kelly Joins the Leafs *33*
Ab Hoffman Fooled Everybody *35*

Death in Minnesota   37
A Moving Tribute to Orr   38
Big Earner, Big Spender   39
Mike Walton: Eccentric on Ice   41
Gretzky Goes to L.A.   42
Phil Esposito's Wild Ride   44
Darryl Sittler's Biggest Night   45
Fast Start, Fast Finish   47
Flight to Freedom   49
Goalie Hextall's Long-shot Goals   50
Thumbs Up for Pat Verbeek   51
The Kid Could Always Score   52
There Was Nobody Like Number Nine   54

PART 2 — Unforgettable Games

Wacky Happenings in Winnipeg   59
The Ice Was Littered with Loot   61
A Bloodbath in Montreal   63
The Curse of Muldoon   64
Suspended — For Life!   66
This Game Was Never Finished   67
The Player in Green   69
Hockey's First Telecast   70
Killer Dill's Comeuppance   71
Was It Murder on Ice?   73
Goal of the Century   74
Pelted with Pucks   76
Strange Objects on the Ice   77
One Hot Dog — To Go   79
Brother against Brother   80
Whenever Kate Warbled the Flyers Won   81

When Francis Fought the Fans   *83*
Why Wait for the Opening Whistle?   *85*

PART 3 — Teams of Fame and Infamy

McGill Boys Organize Hockey   *89*
The End of a Streak   *91*
The All-American Team   *92*
Looking for the Winning Edge   *93*
Worst-Ever Season   *95*
The Flyers' Famous Undefeated Streak   *96*
Miracle on Main Street   *98*
The Homeless Hockey Team   *100*
The Best-Ever Canada Cup   *101*
A Costly Broken Curfew   *103*

PART 4 — Hockey's Supporting Cast

Smythe's Folly   *107*
The Coach Answers the Call   *108*
A Race to The Wire for Clancy   *109*
The Ref's Last Game   *111*
The Original Two-Goalie System   *112*
Eddie Shore's Quirks   *113*
The Eagle and Orr   *115*
Colleen Howe Steps In   *116*
Rebellious George Hayes   *118*
Downfall of an Agent   *119*
Bruins and Rangers Swap All Stars   *121*
The Innovative Roger Neilson   *122*
Rolling in Dough   *124*
The First Goal Nets   *125*

Playoff Fiasco in New Jersey   *127*
Lord Stanley Missed All the Excitement   *128*

PART 5 — Stanley Cup Capers

The Ref Went Home   *131*
The Strangest Cup Challenge   *132*
Ice Hockey or Water Polo?   *134*
Too Many Rings, Not Enough Fingers   *135*
The Cup Was Never Won   *136*
Clancy Did It All   *137*
One Strike and You're Out   *138*
A Tantrum Cost Him the Cup   *140*
The Chicago Cup Caper   *141*
Graybeards Win the Cup   *142*
Adventures of the Stanley Cup   *144*
Secrets of the Cup   *145*
Lafleur Kidnaps the Cup   *147*

PREFACE

EVERYONE INVOLVED IN HOCKEY has a story to tell — stories ranging from tall tales of the Stanley Cup to the captivating story of Abby Hoffman, an eight-year-old girl who masqueraded as a boy and became an all-star on defence.

My good friend the late King Clancy often regaled me with tales of yesterday — how he once played every position in a Stanley Cup game, including that of goaltender! And how, on bitterly cold nights in Ottawa, he and two teammates sat around the stove in the dressingroom playing cards — during games!

Bobby Hull, Harry Neale and Gordie Howe chuckled whenever I asked them about the early seventies and the growing pains of an upstart league — the WHA. Bizarre happenings were commonplace, such as Howe's signing of a million-dollar deal to play with his two sons in Houston and Wayne Gretzky's drawing up of his own contract (in longhand) when he signed with Indianapolis. Not to mention star forward Mike Walton's engaging of a teammate in a fistfight — right on his own team's bench during a game, or the time the Zamboni fell through the ice before the Philadelphia Blazers' home opener.

But this is no place to linger. A lot of my favorite hockey anecdotes lie ahead, waiting for your scrutiny. They are stories collected in dressing rooms, arena corridors, hotel lobbies, sports banquets and while I was on the road playing with the NHL Oldtimers for seventeen memorable years, the only amateur player on the roster. And that's a story in itself — more on that to come, in a later book!

Enjoy!

Special thanks to Wendy Jackson and Rob Granatstein who assisted in the research and to Mark Askin of *Hockey Night in Canada* for his advice and encouragement. Also to Darlene Money, an outstanding editor, and Dick Gibson of the *Toronto Sun*, for his illustrations.

BRIAN MCFARLANE

PART

1

PLAYERS

Bucko the Bodychecker

I T'S AN NHL record you'll never find in any record book — Bucko McDonald's feat of knocking 37 opponents to the ice in one NHL game.

It happened in the Montreal Forum in the 1936 playoffs, in the first game of a series between the Detroit Red Wings and the Montreal Maroons. The Red Wings were relying on their bashing defenceman, Bucko McDonald, a second-year man in the league, to punish the Maroons. The former lacrosse star from Fergus, Ontario loved to hit, and the Maroons were advised to keep their heads up.

Bucko McDonald's pregame meal was a single boiled egg and a dish of ice cream. He'd have eaten a lot more if he'd known he was about to perform in the longest game in NHL history, one that would go into a sixth overtime period. The game began on March 24 and finished in the wee small hours of March 25.

Before the game, a Detroit fan approached Bucko and offered him five dollars for every Maroon he bodychecked to the ice. Of course, the fan never dreamed Bucko would have almost nine periods of hockey — the equivalent of three games — in which to do his body work on the Maroons.

The fan kept score and witnessed 37 crunching checks that sent Maroon forwards sprawling before Bucko's gleeful bashing came to an end. Mud Bruneteau of the Wings scored a dramatic winning goal for Detroit at 2:25 a.m. to end the marathon contest. Bucko collected $185 in "hit" money that night.

"The Maroons became easier to hit as the long overtime wore on," recalls Bucko. "The ice got soft and slushy. They lost their speed, they found it difficult to stay out of my way so I just kept knocking them down."

Bucko McDonald became a member of Parliament after his playing days and a highly regarded coach. In Parry Sound one year, he helped tutor a young phenom named Bobby Orr. It was Bucko who advised Orr's father to let his son play defence. Bucko insisted young Orr was the finest defence prospect he'd ever seen. How right he was. Even though Orr set many records during his NHL career, one he could never top was Bucko's mark — 37 bodychecks in a single game.

How the Habs Got Beliveau

WHEN I WAS A JUNIOR HOCKEY PLAYER for an Ottawa Valley team called the Inkerman Rockets, we sailed through the playoffs one year and had Memorial Cup hopes in mind — until we ran into a powerful team from Quebec named the Citadels.

The Citadels had a marvelous player called Jean Beliveau, and the coach said it was my job to stop him. That, as you may have guessed, was impossible. Our entire team couldn't stop the giant centre.

Beliveau was the best we'd ever seen, and we were certain he would become an instant star with the Montreal Canadiens when he joined them the following year. In that era, before the introduction of the entry draft, NHL teams acquired

4

'HELP YOURSELF, JEAN'

junior players by signing them to "C" forms or by placing their names on a negotiation list. While Beliveau had not signed a "C" form with the Canadiens, his name topped their negotiation list — in capital letters — and this meant he could play for no other professional club.

But Beliveau, to our consternation, spurned a chance to play for the Canadiens. He had been so well treated in Quebec, and so well paid, even as an amateur, that he felt an obligation to his Quebec City fans. Hadn't they filled the new arena in Quebec City to see him play? Hadn't they bought him a new car — a 1951 Nash — and presented it to him during one of the playoff games with Inkerman? Now he would repay them for their support by playing senior hockey for the Quebec City Aces for another year or two.

The Canadiens couldn't stop him because the Quebec Senior League was not a professional league; it was called semipro even though all the players were paid. Beliveau, of course, was paid more than anyone else. For two years he was the Quebec League's biggest star, filling arenas everywhere he played.

Finally, the desperate Canadiens made a bold move. They bought the entire Quebec Senior League and turned it professional. That gave Beliveau little choice but to sign with Montreal. The money he received — a $20,000 bonus and more than $100,000 for a five-year contract — was an enormous sum in those days.

Frank Selke, Sr., then general manager of the Canadiens, was asked what secret he used to land the big centreman. "No secret," he replied with a grin. "I simply opened the Forum vault and said, 'Help yourself, Jean.'"

Montreal fans agreed Beliveau was worth waiting for. He soon became the Habs' most prolific centre and team captain, and helped them win ten Stanley Cups in the next two decades.

Fournier the Fireman

ONE NIGHT BACK IN 1906, fans filled the tiny arena in Buckingham, Quebec for the big game with arch-rival Vankleek Hill. The 400 hometown fans anticipated a victory, perhaps an easy one. Their optimism was based on the play of young Guy Fournier, a local lad who was enjoying an outstanding season in goal.

The fans chanted Fournier's name and jeered the opposing players as the teams skated through the warm-up period. Then, just as the referee was ready to drop the puck, the lights in the arena went out and a cry of "Fire" was heard.

The arena doors were thrown open and the fans rushed into the street. Fortunately, no one was injured in the dash to the exits. A block away, flames could be seen leaping into the sky, consuming the town's only department store. Several fans rushed off to help the fire brigade battle the blaze.

When the fire was finally out, the fans returned to the arena. Some had grimy faces and their clothes smelled of smoke. The hockey players, meanwhile, had been resting in the dark in their dressing rooms, and when electricity was restored, they returned to the ice.

All but one. Goalkeeper Guy Fournier of Buckingham was missing. On learning of the blaze, Fournier, whose father was the town engineer, had raced from the arena still wearing his skates and goal pads. He skated down the snow-packed street to the pump house to help his father keep water flowing to douse the flames. He was gone for more than an hour. He even offered to help get power restored, but his father said, "I'll look after that. You've got a hockey game to play."

It was 9:30 when Fournier arrived back at the rink. The fans gave him a huge ovation. When the referee was finally able to start the match, young Fournier proved he was just as quick in goal as he was in getting to the pump house. He was the number-one star as Buckingham won the game 4–1.

The Player Who Couldn't Score

MANY YEARS AGO when the New York Americans were in the NHL, they had a low-scoring winger on the roster named Eddie Convey. Convey was a buddy of King Clancy, then a star defenceman with the Toronto Maple Leafs.

When Clancy heard that Convey might be sent to the minors if he didn't start producing more goals, he decided to give his old pal some help.

When the Americans played in Toronto one night, Clancy enlisted teammate Charlie Conacher to help him propel their mutual friend Convey into the hockey spotlight. "If you follow the plan I've come up with," Clancy told the obliging Conacher, "Eddie Convey will score at least one goal against us tonight."

Clancy's plan depended on the Leafs gaining a two- or three-goal lead over the Americans. After that Convey would be allowed to sail into the Toronto zone unmolested. "You'll wave at him as he goes by," he told Conacher. "And I'll stumble and fall when I try to check him. I'll leave a big opening, and Eddie will have a perfect chance to go in alone and score."

Sure enough, the Leafs were ahead by three or four goals when Convey zipped around Conacher and flew past the stumbling Clancy. Leaf goalie Lorne Chabot was in on the plan, too. He gave Convey at least half the net for a target. But Convey's shot missed the inviting target and sailed high over the cage.

"Let's give him another chance," suggested Clancy. A few minutes later, Convey again grabbed the rubber and started up the ice. He breezed past Conacher and deked his way past Clancy. Chabot hugged the post, giving Convey even more open net. But did he score? No! This time his rising shot caught Chabot under the chin — right in the Adam's apple.

Chabot fell to the ice, choking and gasping. When Conacher and Clancy arrived on the scene, the goalie glared at them and croaked, "That's enough charity for tonight, fellows. That guy doesn't deserve to score."

Conacher looked at Clancy. "Well, King?"

Clancy growled, "Chabot is right. Next time Convey comes down here, cut his legs out from under him."

Clancy Held a Hot Hand

I often chuckle when I think of an anecdote the late King Clancy once told me about an incident early in his career as a substitute defenceman with the NHL's Ottawa Senators.

"I didn't get much ice time when I first joined the Senators," he said. "Most players were sixty-minute men in those days, so the three Ottawa subs — Morley Bruce, Frank Boucher and I — were used sparingly.

"On bitterly cold nights, the three of us stayed in the dressing room during games. It was a lot warmer in there than on the Ottawa bench. If the coach needed one of us, he simply buzzed the room by pressing a button near the bench. One buzz was for me, two for Bruce and three for Boucher.

"What did we do in there? To tell the truth, we loosened our skates and played cards to pass the time.

"But one night the coach surprised us. He buzzed twice for Bruce, who had his skates off and wasn't ready to play, so Boucher scrambled out in his place. But he was back moments later, saying, 'Coach wants you, Clancy.' Geez, I quickly tied up my laces and hurried out. But there'd been such a delay before I got into the game that everyone was screamin' — the coaches, the players, the fans and the referee.

"It couldn't have happened at a worse time. Wouldn't you know I was holding four aces in my mitts when the buzzer interrupted our card game that night. When I got back to the dressing room I asked my teammates, 'Hey, what happened to the cards I was playing?'"

"Frank Boucher said innocently, 'Why, we put your cards back in the deck. We didn't know when you'd be coming back.'"

"'King, they probably weren't very good cards, anyway,' said Morley. 'Let's deal you some more.'

"I know it's a terrible thing to suspect your teammates of doing anything underhanded, but I can't help but think those two fellows took a little peek at the cards I left on the dressing room table that night.

"And if we did nothing else in that game, we helped to make a little hockey history," Clancy added in conclusion. "Within hours, the league slapped a new rule in the book. From then on, all substitutes were ordered to stay on the bench for the duration of the game, no matter how cold they might get just sitting there."

Bill Barilko's Final Goal

I never knew Bill Barilko but I wish I had. His Toronto Maple Leaf teammates from the fifties — men like Harry Watson, Sid Smith and Howie Meeker — tell me he had style and charisma. On the ice he was tough and fearless. Away from it his blond good looks and sunny disposition captivated everyone.

In the spring of 1951, Barilko was the most popular defenceman on the Toronto team. Called up from the Hollywood Wolves of the Pacific Coast League four years earlier, the cocky rookie from Timmins, Ontario quickly earned a place on the Leaf roster and would not let it go. He was an instant hit with the fans, who loved his enthusiasm, his belligerence and his daring rushes that inevitably wound up in the opposing team's goal mouth.

He didn't score often — only 26 times in 252 regular season games. But one goal he scored, captured in all its beauty through the lens of ace sports photographer Nat Turofsky, will live forever as one of hockey's shining moments. It was the 1951 Stanley Cup winning goal, and sadly, the final goal of Barilko's brief NHL career.

Montreal and Toronto collided in the Stanley Cup finals that season, a thrilling series that lasted five games, every one of them decided in sudden-death overtime. Never before, never since, have all games in a final series required extra time to decide a winner.

The Leafs, on home ice, took a 1–0 lead in the series when rookie Sid Smith scored after 15 seconds of overtime. In game two, also played in Toronto, Montreal superstar Rocket Richard evened matters with a dramatic overtime goal. Despite the split, Toronto had peppered Hab goalie Gerry McNeil with 75 shots in the two games. As a result, the Leafs displayed plenty of confidence as they boarded the train for Montreal and the next two games.

Overtime in game three ended suddenly when Leaf centre Ted Kennedy ripped a long shot past McNeil, and in game four, big Harry Watson scored the overtime winner, to give the Leafs a commanding 3–1 lead in the series.

Back at Maple Leaf Gardens in game five, McNeil's brilliance was a decisive factor in what seemed sure to be a 2–1 Montreal victory. But then leaf coach Joe Primeau pulled goalie Al Rollins from the net with 93 seconds left in regulation time. The strategy paid off when Tod Sloan tied the score, slipping a rebound under McNeil with just 32 seconds on the clock.

Another win in overtime would bring the Stanley Cup to Toronto. Early in the overtime, the Leafs' Howie Meeker gained possession of the puck behind the Montreal net and shoveled it out to the onrushing Bill Barilko.

The big defenceman, never one to hesitate when boldness was called for, galloped in from the blue line and threw his 185-pound body into a desperate shot at McNeil. His aim was true, the red light flashed, and Barilko's dramatic goal won the Stanley Cup for the Leafs.

But there's a sad footnote to this story. A few weeks later, back home in Timmins, Ontario, Barilko and a friend decided to embark on a fly-in fishing trip to the coast of James Bay. Barilko's mother had a premonition something bad might happen and urged him not to go. But he insisted and early on the morning of departure, when he tiptoed into his mother's bedroom and said softly, "Goodbye, Mom," she pretended she didn't hear and refused to answer. It was a decision she would regret for the rest of her life.

The hockey star and his friend flew their small Fairchild pontoon plane to the Seal River, near the northern extremity of James Bay. They fished for two days, caught several dozen trout, which they stored in the pontoons, and started back. After stopping to re-fuel at Rupert House on the southern end of the bay, Barilko's pilot friend had difficulty getting the plane, weighed down with fish, off the water. Finally he succeeded. The plane cleared the treetops and disappeared in the clouds. What happened to the Fairchild and its two occupants after that remains a mystery. One thing soon became clear — the plane went down somewhere between James Bay and Timmins.

Despite a million-dollar search lasting several weeks and covering thousand of miles of bushland, it wasn't till eleven years later that the wreckage of the plane, with skeletal remains of two men inside, was discovered.

Bill Barilko is gone but not forgotten.

The Alfie Moore Saga

IN THE SPRING OF 1937 he was just another goalie, a minor leaguer named Alfie Moore. His season at Pittsburgh was over, and he was back in Toronto, relaxing in a tavern. He wished he had tickets for the big game at the Gardens that night, the first game of the Stanley Cup finals between Chicago and Toronto.

Suddenly two Black Hawk players, Johnny Gottselig and Paul Thompson, burst into the tavern and grabbed Moore. "Come with us," they ordered. "You're playing goal for the Hawks tonight."

It seems Hawks' regular goalie, Mike Karakas, had broken a toe and could not play. When the Hawks pleaded with Leaf owner Conn Smythe to let them use Davie Kerr, a Ranger goalie, Smythe just laughed and said, "No way. Kerr's too good. No, we'll loan you Alfie Moore, our Pittsburgh goalie — that is, if you can find him."

Moore was found, not quite sober perhaps, but eager to play. "I'll show Smythe he made a mistake keeping me in Pittsburgh," he told his new mates.

After giving up an early goal to the Leafs' Gord Drillon, Moore blanked Toronto the rest of the way. Gottselig, who scored twice in the 3–1 Hawk victory, said he could hardly find his name in the paper the next day. All the praise was for Moore.

Smythe was so upset he refused to let Moore play in game two, which the Hawks lost. But at home in

Chicago, with Karakas back in goal, the Hawks won two straight and captured the Stanley Cup.

When the playoff loot was divvied up, the Hawks asked Moore what his services were worth. "Oh, about $150," he said. Bill Tobin, the Hawks' manager, gave Moore twice that amount and later sent him a suitably engraved gold watch.

The legend of Alfie Moore, the goalie they pulled from a tavern, endures to this day.

Stardom Denied

HALF A CENTURY AGO, at 18, Herb Carnegie was a first-rate Junior A player in Toronto, one of the best centre-ice players in the nation. His career led him to the tough Quebec Senior League, then considered to be just one small step below the NHL.

In Quebec, Carnegie became a big star and won three MVP awards. He hoped his hockey skills would lead him to hockey stardom with the New York Rangers — everybody said he had the talent — but the opportunity never came.

Why? Because Carnegie was black. Carnegie knew the odds were against him right from the beginning. As a teenager he'd been told that Conn Smythe, owner of the Leafs, had said of him, "I'd sign him in a minute — if I could only turn him white."

It wasn't until 1958, when the Boston Bruins introduced Willie O'Ree, a rookie from Fredericton, New Brunswick, that a black player cracked the lineup of an NHL team. O'Ree scored four goals in 45 games and was shunted back to the minor leagues.

Blood in Boston

I T HAPPENED on December 12, 1933 at the Boston Garden. The Bruins were playing the Leafs that night and the Leafs, in the second period, were two men short.

Eddie Shore, the Bruins' great defenceman, dashed up the ice and was bowled over in the Leaf zone by King Clancy. Clancy led a return rush, and when he took off, Ace Bailey, one of Toronto's best forwards, stepped around the fallen Shore and took Clancy's place on the Leaf blue line.

Just then, Shore jumped up and charged Bailey from behind, sending the Leaf player flying with a vicious check. Bailey's head hit the ice with a crack that could be heard throughout the arena.

Red Horner of the Leafs retaliated at once. He smashed Shore in the face and knocked him out with one punch. Now there were two bodies on the ice, two heads oozing blood.

When Bailey was carried off the ice on a stretcher, a Bruin fan taunted Leaf owner Conn Smythe. Smythe lashed out, struck the fan and more blood flowed. Smythe was arrested by Boston police and thrown in jail.

With his skull fractured in two places, Bailey was rushed to hospital, where a team of brain surgeons tried desperately to save his life. Somehow he survived two major operations, but his hockey career ended that night.

Bailey's father, who had been listening to the game on radio back in Toronto, left hurriedly for Boston, packing a gun. He had every intention of

16

shooting the player who had ended his son's career. Luckily he was intercepted in Boston by Leaf officials, who spiked his drink and placed the groggy father of the stricken star on a train back to Toronto.

Shore was vilified in the press and suspended for a month. But one man who never berated Shore was Bailey, the victim of his attack. Later that season, a benefit game was held for Bailey in Toronto — the first all-star game in NHL history — and when the two stars, Bailey and Shore, shook hands at centre ice, they received a deafening ovation.

Brimsek's Brilliance

NO ROOKIE GOALIE ever got off to a better start in the NHL than a kid from Minnesota named Frankie Brimsek. On December 1, 1938, the Boston Bruins started Brimsek in goal against the Montreal Canadiens at the Forum. The Bruins claimed Brimsek would make everyone forget their former netminder, the great Tiny Thompson, who'd been sold to Detroit for $15,000. The Boston players doubted it, for Thompson, a ten-year veteran, had won four Vezina trophies and was extremely popular. Dit Clapper, Thompson's roommate, was so upset at the goalie's departure he threatened to quit hockey.

Brimsek, aware he was replacing a Bruin immortal, was cool, quick and unflappable in his debut against Montreal. Still, the Bruins lost 2–0.

But in the next seven games Brimsek played his way out from under Thompson's huge shadow and into a spotlight of his own creation. He went into Chicago and shut out the Black Hawks 4–0. Two nights later, he shut them out again, this time 2–0. He followed up with a third straight shutout, a 3–0 whitewashing of the Rangers. In game five he broke Thompson's Boston record for shutout minutes as the Bruins edged Montreal 3–2. Until Montreal scored, Brimsek had gone 231 minutes and 54 seconds without allowing a goal.

In his next three games, he was perfect again. He blanked the Canadiens 1–0, the Red Wings 2–0 and the New York Americans 2–0 — three more shutouts for the Bruin rookie, who was already being called Mr. Zero.

It couldn't last forever. The Rangers finally snapped his second shutout streak with a 1–0 victory. But what a start for rookie Brimsek! Six shutouts in his first eight games. No wonder he went on to win the rookie award (with ten shutouts and a 1.59 goals-against average), the Vezina Trophy and a berth on the first all-star team.

Thanks to Brimsek's sensational netminding, the Bruins swept to the Stanley Cup finals against Toronto. Mr. Zero gave up a mere six goals to the Leafs in the final series, and the Bruins captured the Cup four games to one.

The Stingiest Goalie

GEORGE HAINSWORTH of the Montreal Canadiens set a remarkable NHL record during the 1928–29 season. He recorded 22 shutouts in 44 games. What's more, he allowed only 43 goals in the 44 games he played.

"Sudden Death" Hill

When Mel Hill, a 140-pound right winger from Glenboro, Manitoba tried out for the New York Rangers in the mid-1930s, he was rejected. Too light, they said. So Hill played amateur hockey for a year, added some weight and was good enough to catch on as a regular with the Boston Bruins in the 1938–39 season.

But the rookie didn't score very often — no goals at all by Christmas, and only ten for the entire regular season. With first-team all-stars Eddie Shore and Dit Clapper on defence, and high-scoring forward Bill Cowley (league MVP and scoring champion), Milt Schmidt, Bobby Bauer, Porky Dumart and Roy Conacher up front, Hill soon became accustomed to playing in the shadow of more talented players. Indeed, he considered himself fortunate to be able to cling to a spot on the Bruin roster.

But in the 1939 playoffs, Hill stood out like a beacon. Boston met New York in the first round, and rookie Hill scored a dramatic winning goal in game one after almost three periods (59 minutes, 25 seconds) of overtime. It was 1.10 a.m. when Hill's shot ended proceedings. In game two, he scored again in overtime to give the Bruins their second straight victory.

The Bruins won game three in regulation time, but the Rangers fought back with three straight victories, forcing a seventh and deciding game at the Boston Garden. The score there was tied 1–1 at the end of regulation time, and the first overtime period was scoreless. So was the second.

19

Late in the third overtime, Bill Cowley threw a pass from the corner onto Hill's stick and Mel slapped it past Ranger goalie Davie Kerr to win the game and end the series. The red light flashed after 48 minutes of extra time. With three overtime winners, Hill acquired the nickname Sudden Death, a monicker that stuck to him for the rest of his life. When fans sought his autograph, they even asked him to preface his name with "Sudden Death."

Hill's Bruins went on to win the Stanley Cup that spring with a final series' triumph over Toronto. Hill's bonus money, $2000 for the Cup win and a special bonus of $1000 for the three overtime goals, equaled his $3,000 regular-season salary.

Cool Head, Nervous Stomach

DURING WORLD WAR TWO good goalies were scarce, but the Toronto Maple Leafs came up with a stellar stopper in Frank McCool. There was just one problem with McCool. He had ulcers. When he faced the pressure of playoff hockey, his ulcers flared up and made every game a painful experience.

In the spring of 1945, the Leafs managed to reach the Stanley Cup finals, even though they'd finished 28 points behind first-place Montreal in regular-season play. It was considered a stunning upset when the Leafs eliminated the Habs in six games in the semifinals. Montreal had lost only eight games all season, and the Canadiens' famed Punch Line of Toe Blake, Rocket Richard and Elmer Lach had finished one, two, three in the NHL scoring race.

Playing a large role in the upset was rookie netminder Frank McCool, whose nervous stomach made playoff competition an agonizing experience. Each pressure-packed game brought him to the brink of collapse.

Now the Leafs prepared to meet a strong Detroit team in the Cup finals. Despite their dramatic win over Montreal, no one figured the Leafs for a second straight upset — not with a sick and inexperienced goaltender carrying their Stanley Cup hopes. There was concern that McCool, unable to cope with the stomach pain that plagued him, might have to be replaced.

But McCool was magnificent in game one and stopped Detroit 1–0. In game two he came up with another shutout, this time 2–0. In game three he blanked the Red Wings again. Three games, three shutouts and a record for stinginess unequaled in postseason play.

Between games, and between periods of each game, McCool soothed his flaming ulcers by drinking plenty of milk.

Then, with the Stanley Cup almost within his grasp, he faltered. The Red Wings stopped his shutout streak after 193 minutes (a playoff record), staving off elimination with a 5–3 triumph in game four. They used McCool's own weapon, the shutout, to stop the Leafs in games five and six.

By then the rookie's stomach was on fire and his confidence sagging fast. His chance to win the Stanley Cup appeared to be slipping away.

Game seven quickly heaped more pressure on McCool's shoulders as neither team was able to score. The most important game of the year remained scoreless for over two periods. Midway through the third, with the score tied 1–1, McCool's ulcers almost knocked him right out of the game.

He doubled over in the Leaf net, then pleaded with the referee for time out in order to take some stomach medicine.

Today, he would be denied a respite, and a back-up goalie would come off the bench to replace him. But in that era there were no backups. Every goalie was a sixty-minute man. So McCool got the break he requested and left the ice. He spent ten minutes in the dressing room sipping milk to soothe his ulcer pangs.

Soon after he returned, the Leafs' Babe Pratt scored the game-winning goal and Toronto won the Stanley Cup with a 2–1 victory. McCool, with four playoff shutouts, had played the best hockey of his career while suffering almost unbearable pain.

The following season, McCool shared the Leaf goaltending job with returned war veteran Turk Broda. The 1945 playoff hero played in 22 games, failed to collect another shutout and quickly faded from the NHL scene. But "Ulcers" McCool left behind an enviable record — three consecutive shutouts in the Stanley Cup playoffs.

A Fast Start

SITTING ACROSS THE NHL Oldtimers' dressing room from me, Gus Bodnar stopped lacing his skates and took a minute to tell me about the fall of 1943 when, as an 18-year-old rookie, he journeyed from his home in Thunder Bay (then Fort William) to try out with the Leafs.

"When I arrived at training camp, Bucko McDonald, a veteran defenceman, took me aside

22

and gave me two bits of advice. 'Keep your head up, kid, and get your hair cut.'

"Well, I got the haircut and I managed to keep my head up often enough to score a few goals in the scrimmages, and coach Hap Day decided I was good enough to play on his hockey club. There I was in the Leaf starting lineup on opening night. I remember it was October 30, 1943. Naturally I was anxious to play, but I hadn't expected the coach to send me out to take the opening faceoff against the New York Rangers.

"Everything was a blur after that. Seconds after the puck was dropped I found myself going in all alone on Ranger goalie Ken McAuley, who was also a rookie. Somehow I shot the puck past him. I'd scored after just 15 seconds of play, on my first shift, on my very first NHL shot. That's a record that has lasted almost 50 years. And poor McAuley, in the same time span, gave up his first NHL goal, which may have been a record, too.

"Even today, half a century later, I can hardly believe I scored that goal. But I know I did because my name is still in the NHL record book. It says: Fastest goal by a rookie, Gus Bodnar of Toronto, in 15 seconds. The closest anyone ever came to matching my mark was when Danny Gare of Buffalo scored after 18 seconds in his first shift. That was in 1974.

"The day after I scored the goal in 15 seconds, the lady who owned the boardinghouse I was staying in baked a big cake for me in recognition of my achievement. My teammates and I demolished that cake in minutes, even though our coach had strict rules about eating too much rich heavy food.

"I went on to play 12 seasons in the NHL with three different teams, but of all the exciting things that happened to me over those years, few can top my first 15 seconds on the ice."

Sawchuk's Dazzling Playoffs

ASK ANY OLD-TIME HOCKEY BROADCASTER to name the greatest goalie he's ever seen and chances are he'll tell you it's Terry Sawchuk. One of Sawchuk's remarkable records — 103 shutouts in a 20-year NHL career — may never be broken.

It was shutout goaltending that made Sawchuk famous back in 1952 when he was a second-year man with the Detroit Red Wings. In 1951, having captured the Calder Trophy as top rookie and having been named to the all-star team, he'd already established himself as one of the best netminders in the game. But nobody expected him to be almost flawless when the Wings met Toronto in the playoffs in 1952.

Sawchuk blanked the Leafs in the first two games 3–1 and 1–0, and allowed only 3 Toronto goals in the next two games (6–2 and 3–1 for Detroit). The Red Wings skated off with a four-game sweep of the semifinals.

The young goalie was just as hot against powerful Montreal when the final series opened at the Montreal Forum. Sawchuk gave up a single goal in game one and another lone score in game two. Both games went to Detroit, 3–1 and 2–1. Back on home ice, Sawchuk was even stingier. He chalked up two straight shutouts with identical 3–0 scores.

Reporters agreed it was Sawchuk's brilliance that enabled the Red Wings to become the first team in history to sweep eight straight games en route to the Cup.

In the eight games, Sawchuk recorded four shutouts. He gave up a mere five goals and his goals-against average was an incredible 0.62. No playoff goaltender has come close to matching that performance.

The Winnipeg native went on to other Cup triumphs — two more with Detroit in 1954 and 1955 and one with Toronto in 1967. But the Stanley Cup playoff that pleased him the most was the eight-game sweep in the spring of '52.

Battle of the Bulge

IN THE LATE 1940S AND EARLY 1950S fat and funny Turk Broda of the Toronto Maple Leafs was one of the most popular players in the NHL. He led the Leafs to four Stanley Cups in the '40s and another in 1951. Old-timers say he was one of the greatest "money" goalies in hockey.

But none of Broda's countless fans will ever forget a week in November 1949 when Leaf owner Conn Smythe demanded that the goalie reduce his waistline . . . or else. Broda weighed 197 pounds at the time, and Smythe decreed publicly, "My goalie's too fat. He'd better lose seven pounds before the next game or I'll be looking for another goalie."

To show he meant business, Smythe recalled goalie Gilles Mayer from the Leaf farm club in Pittsburgh, where Mayer, a skinny kid, was drinking milkshakes trying to gain weight.

FOUR MORE... THREE MORE... TWO MORE...

So began the famous Battle of the Bulge. Broda went on a crash diet and lost four pounds the very first day. All of Canada got caught up in the story. Papers carried photos of Broda emerging from a steam room, Broda nibbling on celery sticks, Broda lifting weights in the Leaf dressing room.

The weigh-in was set for Saturday afternoon, just before a big game with the New York Rangers. When Broda stepped on the scales, the needle settled just under 190. He'd made it! Canadians from coast to coast breathed a little easier, and the grinning goaltender accepted congratulations from friends and teammates.

When the slimmed-down netminder skated onto the ice that night, he received a tremendous ovation from his fans. The regimental band at the Gardens played "Happy Days Are Here Again" and followed up with a chorus of "She's Too Fat For Me."

Broda rewarded his supporters in the best possible way, by chalking up a shutout over the visiting Rangers.

One of Hockey's Oldest Records

ON MARCH 12, 1912, defenceman Frank Patrick of Vancouver scored a phenomenal six goals from his defence position in a game against New Westminster. This record has never been matched.

A Million for Mahovlich

IT WAS OCTOBER, 1962. Harold Ballard, who, along with Stafford Smythe and John Bassett, had recently bought the Toronto Maple Leafs from Conn Smythe, was having a drink or two with Chicago Black Hawks owner Jim Norris at the Royal York Hotel in Toronto.

Although the Hawks had won the Stanley Cup the preceding year, with Bobby Hull leading the way, Norris had his eye on another great left-winger. The man he had in mind was the Leafs' young star Frank Mahovlich. What a pair! The Big M and the Golden Jet. Norris knew the Leafs were having difficulty signing Mahovlich. Maybe he could be pried loose with a bundle of cash.

His hunch was accurate. Several drinks later a deal was made. The Leafs agreed to sell Mahovlich to Chicago for a record price — one million dollars.

Ballard and Norris shook hands on the deal, and Norris handed Ballard a one-thousand-dollar bill as a deposit.

Next morning came and there were sober second thoughts — not in the Chicago camp but in Toronto. Former Leaf owner Conn Smythe told his son Stafford the deal was ridiculous — it was bad for hockey. Many others agreed, including thousands of Leaf fans once the news leaked out.

Meanwhile, Chicago general manager Tommy Ivan wasted no time attempting to finalize arrangements. He hurried to the Gardens to deliver a cheque to the Leafs in the amount of one million dollars.

At an emergency meeting of Leaf executives a lot of emotional voices were raised. Then Stafford Smythe emerged and sheepishly announced, "Frank Mahovlich is not for sale. Not at any price. The money is going back."

When asked to comment, Jim Norris said angrily, "Toronto welched on the deal."

Oh, Brother

IN AT LEAST ONE NHL GAME, played in Chicago on December 1, 1940, there were four sets of brothers on the ice. Lynn and Muzz Patrick and Neil and Mac Colville played for the Rangers; Max and Doug Bentley and Bill and Bob Carse were in uniform for the Black Hawks.

Baun Scores the Winner — On a Broken Leg

FORMER LEAF STALWART BOBBY BAUN doesn't play old-timers' hockey with us anymore — his doctor advised against it because of a broken neck the hard-rock defenceman suffered in an NHL game an injury that ended his career. We miss the man who is often asked about his biggest moment in hockey — the time he scored a winning playoff goal while skating on a broken leg.

Baun's memorable moment came in 1964 in Detroit, in the sixth game of the final series between the Leafs and the Red Wings. If the Wings won they would capture the Stanley Cup. With the score tied 3–3, Gordie Howe of the Wings rifled a shot that caught Baun just above the ankle. The Leaf defenceman had to be carried off on a stretcher.

In the dressing room, Baun had local anesthetic injected in the ankle to kill the pain, and when the game went into overtime, there he was back on the ice.

After one minute and 43 seconds of overtime, Baun took a pass from Bob Pulford and slapped the puck at Red Wings netminder Terry Sawchuk. The disk deflected off Detroit defenceman Bill Gadsby and found the net for the winning goal. In 55 previous playoff games, Baun had scored only twice.

So it was back to Toronto for the seventh and deciding game. Baun disregarded doctors' advice to have his aching leg x-rayed. "Later," he said, "I'll do it later. Look after Kelly, Brewer and Mahovlich first." Leaf centre Red Kelly was nursing sprained knee ligaments, defenceman Carl Brewer had a rib separation, and left-winger Frank Mahovlich had a bruised shoulder.

For the final game, Baun's leg was once again injected with painkiller. He played a regular shift despite severe pain. It wasn't until the Leafs won the game 4–0 and had the Stanley Cup firmly in their grasp that he consented to have his leg x-rayed. The medical technicians confirmed what Baun already suspected. A cast would be needed for the leg he'd broken a couple of nights earlier.

An Unbeatable Goaltending Streak

IN MODERN-DAY HOCKEY, when NHL teams use two, three, four or even five goalies in a season, it's hard to believe that just a few years ago teams relied on one man, and one man only, to guard their nets.

And no team relied on a netminder more than Chicago in the sixties when Glenn Hall toiled for the Windy City club. Game in and game out, Hall was always there. He played three, four, five hundred games in a row. Remember, this was in the era before the face mask, when all goaltenders suffered frequent cuts and concussions.

On the night of November 7, 1962, Chicago was at home to Boston. And Hall wasn't feeling well. Of course, nobody expected him to feel well; his penchant for throwing up before games and between periods was widely publicized. Similarly his habit of wrestling with the team trainer for several minutes in an effort to settle his pregame nerves had become a familiar ritual.

But on this night there was no wrestling in the dressing room. Hall's physical problems wouldn't allow it, for they were far worse than a nervous stomach. The pain in his lower back was excruciating. A lesser athlete wouldn't have thought of suiting up for the game. But when the Hawks took the ice that night, Hall was standing calmly between the pipes as usual. It was his 503rd consecutive game, or his 552nd counting playoffs.

The game was only a few minutes old when Boston's Murray Oliver shot the puck at Hall and it flew right between his legs. Hall's back pain was so intense that he simply hadn't been able to bend over to block the puck the way he normally would have. It was impossible for him to carry on in goal.

Hall skated slowly to the Hawk bench, said a few words to his coach and then moved on to the dressing room, ending more than 33,000 consecutive minutes of goaltending in his 503rd game.

The most fantastic iron-man streak in professional sport was finally over.

Goalies Are Different

GOALIES AREN'T AT ALL LIKE the other players on a hockey team. They not only use different skates, pads and sticks but they act differently.

Look at one of the all-time best — Georges Vezina, after whom the Vezina Trophy is named. Vezina enjoyed playing goal in his street shoes until he was in his late teens. He'd probably have played in the NHL that way if the Montreal Canadiens had let him.

Another early-day goalie was Percy LeSueur from Ottawa. He used the same goal stick for every league and playoff game for five straight seasons. There was fat Billy Nicholson, too, a 300-pounder who astonished everyone early in the century by rambling up the ice and attempting to score goals. Fred Brophy of Montreal Westmount became the first goalie to race down the ice and score a goal in 1905.

Goalie Fred Chittick, an Ottawa star in 1898, refused to play in a Stanley Cup playoff game because management wouldn't cough up a "fair number" of complimentary tickets to a big game.

In the NHL, Montreal's Bill Durnan was amazingly ambidextrous. He often switched his big goal stick from hand to hand, thoroughly confusing opposing forwards.

Gary "Suitcase" Smith, who played with eight different NHL teams, used to strip off his uniform between periods of each game. Teammates marveled at the energy he put into taking off 30 pounds of gear, then putting it all back on again. Early in his career, Smith wore as many as 13 pairs of socks under his goal skates. Smith also developed a unique habit of drop-kicking the puck a hundred feet down the ice after making a save.

Ken Dryden quit the Montreal Canadiens one year to earn $135 a week with a Toronto law firm. Boston's Gerry Cheevers painted stitch marks on his goal mask as a reminder of what might have happened to his face if the mask hadn't been there. Jacques Plante, who introduced the face mask to NHL hockey, was an excellent knitter and used to knit toques and other garments to pass the time on road trips.

Gilles Gratton had some interesting quirks. He once streaked across the ice naked and was a firm believer in reincarnation. "In Biblical days I stoned people to death," he would say. "Now they are repaying me by hurling pucks at my head."

Glenn Hall, who played a record 502 consecutive games in the NHL, says he threw up before every one of them. "And often between periods, too," he adds.

In 1987, Philadelphia's Ron Hextall duplicated Brophy's turn-of-the-century feat and fulfilled a lifelong ambition by scoring a goal — from goal line to goal line against the Boston Bruins. Later, he scored another in a playoff game.

Who says goalies are just like the other players on a team?

Kelly Joins the Leafs

LIKABLE RED KELLY was an outstanding defenceman with the Detroit Red Wings in the 1950s. He skated on eight championship teams and four Stanley Cup winners. He won the Lady Byng Trophy for gentlemanly play four times and was a six-time all-star. Kelly was so good and so popular, it looked as if he'd spend his entire career in a Detroit uniform.

But during the 1959–60 season, his 13th as a Red Wing, Kelly heard rumors that Detroit manager Jack Adams thought he was all washed up. A few days later, Adams shocked the hockey establishment by trading Kelly — along with Billy

33

McNeill — to the Rangers, in return for Bill Gadsby and Eddie Shack.

What Adams didn't count on was a huge stubborn streak in Kelly's Irish makeup. The redhead talked things over with his wife, Andra, then called Adams and politely told him the deal was unacceptable. He had no intention of reporting to New York. In fact, if need be, he'd retire from hockey before joining the Rangers. So the deal with New York was called off.

League President Clarence Campbell, disturbed at Kelly's attitude, advised the defenceman he had five days to report to New York or his name would be placed on the retirement list. "You'll be blackballed from hockey forever," warned Campbell. Two days before Campbell's deadline, Kelly received a call from King Clancy in Toronto.

"Red, how'd you like to play for Toronto?" asked Clancy, a fellow Irishman. Leaf manager Punch Imlach believed in veteran players, and Kelly, at 32, would fit right into Imlach's system. Kelly was swayed by Clancy's persuasive blarney and said he would be happy to wind down his career in Toronto. Imlach got on the phone to Adams, and dispatched a journeyman defenceman, Marc Reaume, to Detroit in return for a player who was far from washed up. In fact, some of Kelly's greatest seasons were still ahead of him.

When Kelly joined the Leafs there was another surprise in store for him. Imlach said, "Forget about defence. You're going to be my number one centreman." Imlach gave him two big wingers, Frank Mahovlich and Bob Nevin, and the trio clicked immediately.

With Kelly at centre, the Leafs won four Stanley Cups in the next seven years. The defenceman-turned-forward not only won championships, he combined hockey with politics and served as a member of Parliament while he played for the Leafs. Eventually, he even became their coach.

Ab Hoffman Fooled Everybody

THOUSANDS OF GIRLS PLAY organized hockey, and thousands of women register with hockey associations every year. In 1990 a team of Canadian women won the world's title in Ottawa, defeating the United States in a thrilling championship game. The next showcase for women's hockey could be the Olympic Games — as a demonstration sport initially.

Even though girls and women have been playing hockey for a hundred years, it has traditionally been a game where men and boys come first.

Back in 1955, eight-year-old Abigail Hoffman of Toronto took a good look at organized hockey and decided that girls weren't getting a fair chance to participate in this fast-moving game. Abby had played a lot of hockey with her brothers down at the corner rink, and she figured she was just as clever on skates as most of the boys in her age bracket. So she signed up as a player in the Toronto Hockey League as Ab Hoffman, defence.

And what a player Ab turned out to be! At the end of the season, the league officials named Ab to the all-star team. However, a routine check of Ab's birth certificate revealed an oddity. "He" was said to be a female. "No one noticed it earlier," said Earl Graham, the league chairman. "It knocked the wind out of us when we discovered Ab was a girl. Her birth certificate was mixed in with about 400 others, and nobody even thought about checking gender."

Suddenly, Abby's secret was out. And just as suddenly, she became a celebrity. Her story was in all the papers. She was interviewed on radio and television. She received invitations to see NHL games at the Montreal Forum and Maple Leaf Gardens.

Nobody tried to bar her from hockey. She kept on playing with her team — the Tee Pees — and was a popular member of the club. "She sure fooled us all, but we want her to stay with us," said teammate Russ Turnbull. "She's really good."

After two seasons in boys' hockey, Abby joined a girls' team. But she found it less exciting. So she quit the game and went on to excel in other sports, first swimming, then track and field. In time she became a world-class runner and competed in two Olympics. In 1972, she captured a bronze medal in the women's 800 at the Olympic Games in Munich, West Germany. Now retired from active competition in athletics, she serves as Director of Sport Canada.

But she'll always be remembered as the girl hockey player who fooled everybody.

Death in Minnesota

NHL EXPANSION IN 1967 made it possible for dozens of players to fulfill their dreams of playing hockey at the highest level. One of these players was Bill Masterton, a Winnipeg native.

In the early sixties, Masterton had played with Cleveland in the American League. But he decided to quit pro hockey and return to university when none of the six NHL teams showed much interest in him. After graduating from Denver University with a master's degree he was hired by the Honeywell Corporation in Minneapolis. He considered pro hockey part of his past, and his future looked bright in the corporate world. From now on, he figured, he'd just play hockey on weekends — for fun.

Then came NHL expansion and a doubling of the league from six to twelve teams. The new clubs looked everywhere for talent, and someone in the Minnesota organization recommended Masterton. He hadn't been out of the game very long, he was still fairly young and he'd kept himself in top condition.

The North Stars contacted Masterton and suggested he give hockey one more whirl. Masterton couldn't resist. He agreed to a tryout and easily made the team. That was the end of his career with Honeywell.

On January 13, 1968, the 29-year-old rookie was playing against the Oakland Seals when he was checked by two tough defencemen, Ron Harris and Larry Cahan. Off balance, Masterton tumbled to the ice, struck his head and was knocked unconscious. He was rushed to hospital, but died two days later of massive brain damage.

Bill Masterton was the first and only player to die of an on-ice injury since the league was formed in 1917.

A Moving Tribute to Orr

THAT JANUARY NIGHT IN 1979 was a night to remember at the Boston Garden. The Bruins were entertaining a team of touring Soviets. But the visiting team wasn't the reason this game was a hotter ticket than any Stanley Cup final.

The occasion was Bobby Orr Night, with starting time postponed for 30 memorable pregame minutes while friends and fans honored the greatest Bruin of them all.

Play-by-play broadcaster Bob Cole and I sat in our cramped booth above the ice, all but deafened by wave after wave of applause and the din of the cheering. The thunderous ovation went on and on and on . . . and rose to a peak when at centre ice, Bobby Orr, with his wife Peggy by his side, took off his suit jacket and slipped on his famous number-4 jersey.

No Bruin, no player anywhere, ever did the things that Orr did on ice. He scored 264 goals in a ten-year career and twice led the NHL in scoring. One year he collected 135 points . . . this at a time when 100-point seasons were not as common as they are today.

Orr won the Norris Trophy eight straight times, the Hart Trophy as MVP three times, and he was a perennial first-team all-star.

Almost single-handedly he took the Bruins from last place to first in the NHL standings and pushed them to two Stanley Cups. He revolutionized hockey with his rushing, offensive style, and he did all this while playing on a gimpy left knee that required six operations and forced him out of hockey much, much too soon.

In the Boston Garden that night, a banner was raised in Bobby Orr's honor. His name and number were on the banner and the years he served the Bruins so well — 1966–76. Boston management had let him slip away to Chicago for a couple of years — a big mistake — but now he was back, back to stay if not to play.

With their prolonged ovation, Bobby's fans let him know how much they appreciated all he had done for them, and how much they loved him.

Big Earner, Big Spender

LAWYER BOB WOOLF, who at one time represented several famous athletes, once said, "Getting big money for hockey players isn't difficult. Getting them to hang on to their money is the big problem." Woolf knows from experience. One of his clients, Derek Sanderson, ranks as the all-time money spender in hockey history.

In 1972, the Philadelphia Blazers of the WHA lured Sanderson away from the Boston Bruins with a five-year $2.65 million-dollar contract. At $500,000 a year, Sanderson was regarded as the most highly paid athlete in the world.

But after the first few games of the 1972 season, and a series of injuries that kept their star out of the lineup, the Blazers wanted out of the contract. They paid Sanderson another million to forget the whole deal.

What happened to that money? Sanderson told me once he doesn't remember. "But there are a lot of things I don't remember from that time in my life," he added.

Someone once estimated Sanderson earned over $333,000 for each goal he scored in Philadelphia. During his ten-year career he grossed almost $2 million. But he spent the money as fast as it came in. On wine and women. On a trip to Hawaii, a Rolls-Royce. He'd buy new golf clubs, and after a single round, give them to the caddy. He'd lend money to friends and forget to ask for it back. He figures he may simply have blown $600,000 while drifting from team to team.

When his playing days were over, there was no money left.

Today, Sanderson has his life in order. He works as a commentator on Boston Bruins game broadcasts, and he's respected as a hardworking, clean-living individual who always has time to speak against drug and alcohol abuse to impressionable teenagers.

Mike Walton: Eccentric on Ice

WHEN MIKE WALTON retired from pro hockey a few years ago to enter the real estate business, he left behind a legacy of bizarre behavior in hockey.

Early in his career with the Toronto Maple Leafs, Walton showed up at Maple Leaf Gardens one night wearing a Beatles wig — his way of protesting coach Punch Imlach's ban on long hair and sideburns.

Broadcaster Harry Neale, who coached Walton when both were with Minnesota in the WHA, recalls the time Mike skated off the ice after a game with Houston. Instead of turning into the Minnesota dressing room to shower and change, Walton clomped across the cement floor toward the parking lot, jumped in his car and disappeared into the night. An hour later, according to one witness, Walton was spotted at his favorite bar, nursing a beer and still wearing his hockey uniform.

On a road trip, Neale had scheduled a practice session for his team in a suburban arena outside Winnipeg. Right next to the arena — as part of a sports complex — was a swimming pool. When the Minnesota players passed the pool en route to their dressing room, they saw a familiar figure waving at them through the large panes of glass. There was Mike Walton, perched on the high board and dressed in his full hockey uniform. His swan dive into the pool earned him a round of applause and a perfect 10 from his astonished mates, but with all that gear on, he almost drowned trying to get back to the surface.

Interviewed on television one night, Mike startled the host of the show by appearing naked, covered only in gobs of shaving cream.

Midway through a game in Minnesota, Neale couldn't believe his eyes. He looked down at his bench to see Walton engaged in a fistfight with Gord Gallant, one of his teammates. Neale had never before seen two teammates throwing punches at each other in the middle of a game. When the referee came over to investigate, Neale told the official, "Look, you can't give them penalties. They're both on the same side."

When Walton's play improved after the altercation with Gallant, Neale told his players, "Look, if you want to wake Mike up, take a poke at him."

Gretzky Goes to L.A.

IN JUNE 1988, when the Edmonton Oilers were celebrating their fourth Stanley Cup victory, team captain Wayne Gretzky said he'd like to be around to celebrate ten more Stanley Cups as an Oiler. Two months later, Gretzky was gone from Edmonton, traded by the Oilers to the Los Angeles Kings in a blockbuster deal that stunned hockey fans everywhere.

Oiler fans were shocked and furious. They needed someone to blame because they felt they'd been robbed of a priceless possession. Some of them blamed Wayne's wife, American actress Janet Jones. They called her Jezebel and Yoko Ono and said she'd persuaded Wayne to leave for Hollywood. Others blamed the greed of Oiler owner Peter Pocklington.

Pocklington claimed that Bruce McNall, the dynamic new owner of the Kings, had approached him during the summer and asked what it would take to get Wayne. Pocklington said he would never have considered dealing his superstar if Wayne hadn't called him to say he wanted to move on. It's true that Wayne expressed an interest in the Kings, saying, "It would be beneficial for everyone involved to let me play for Los Angeles."

But Eddie Mio and Paul Coffey, Wayne's best friends, said Wayne was devastated at the thought of leaving the Oilers. Coffey said, "There's no bloody way he wanted to leave. I don't care if he married the Queen of England." Mio added, "It was only after the papers were drawn up that Wayne decided he'd had enough of Peter Pocklington. And nobody should blame Janet for this move. She does not deserve to be persecuted . . . not for a minute."

The terms of the deal? Gretzky, along with Marty McSorley, Mike Krushelnyski and minor leaguer John Miner to the Kings, in return for Jimmy Carson, Martin Gelinas, the Kings' first-round draft choice in 1988, three first-round choices in '89, and '91 and '93, the rights to minor-leaguer Craig Redmond, plus 15 million dollars.

No matter who's to blame or who won the deal, there's never been a trade like it. Not in hockey, not in any sport.

'SIGNAL A LEFT PHIL'

Phil Esposito's Wild Ride

IN THE SPRING OF 1973, the Boston Bruins were knocked out of the Stanley Cup playoffs by the New York Rangers. During the series, Bruins' star Phil Esposito was nailed by a Ron Harris check and taken to a Boston hospital, where doctors diagnosed torn knee ligaments. The star centreman's leg was encased in a cast to protect the injury.

When the Boston players decided to hold a postseason farewell party, one of them suggested that the affair "just wouldn't be the same without Esposito, our team leader." The others agreed.

The NHL scoring champ had to be present, even if he made only a token appearance. So they went to the hospital to get him.

While two of the Bruins, posing as security men, distracted hospital personnel, several other players stealthily wheeled Esposito, still in his hospital bed, along a corridor, down an elevator and through an exit. Unfortunately, in the haste of their daring departure, they broke a metal railing.

The bed and its famous occupant flew down the avenue while car horns honked and pedestrians gawked. The Bruins, led by Wayne Cashman and Bobby Orr, wheeled their leader to a restaurant not far from the hospital. At one busy corner, Orr yelled, "Signal a left, Phil," and Espo's arm shot out from under the sheets.

After the party, Espo was wheeled back to the hospital. But officials there were not amused at the kidnapping of their famous patient. The Bruins were not only chastised for their behavior, they were presented with a bill charging them $400 for damage to hospital property.

They dealt with the bill in a predictable manner. While Espo slept, his mates quietly slipped the invoice under his pillow.

Darryl Sittler's Biggest Night

WHEN TORONTO HOSTED BOSTON in a game at Maple Leaf Gardens on February 7, 1976, the fans anticipated some sparkling performances . . . especially from the Bruins. Coached by colorful Don Cherry, the

45

Bruins were looking for their eighth straight win and veteran centre Jean Ratelle was looking for a milestone goal — his 350th. Forty-year-old left-winger Johnny Bucyk was on the verge of moving into second place on the all-time point-scoring list, and there was even a chance that goalie Gerry Cheevers, lured back to Boston from the WHA a day or two earlier, would be the Bruins' starting goaltender.

What the fans didn't anticipate was a record-smashing performance from a Leaf — captain Darryl Sittler who embarked on a scoring rampage unequaled in the more than 13,000 games played in the NHL up to that night.

Moments before our *Hockey Night in Canada* telecast on the CBC that night, play-by-play announcer Bill Hewitt and I were surprised to learn that Cheevers would not be the Bruins' goaltender. Don Cherry handed the starting assignment to a kid out of college, rookie netminder Dave Reece.

During the game, Ratelle succeeded in scoring his milestone goal, and Bucyk, with two points, moved ahead of Alex Delvecchio and into second place (behind Gordie Howe) on the list of all-time career-point scorers.

But by then, any Bruin scoring feats had been completely overshadowed by Darryl Sittler's incredible performance. The Leaf captain demolished Reece and the Bruins, collecting a record ten points in Toronto's 11–4 romp. He broke by two points the previous record held by a pair of Canadiens, Rocket Richard and Bert Olmstead.

Sittler, then at the peak of his playing career, scored three goals against Reece in the second period and three more in the third to become the first in the NHL to score three goals in each of consecutive periods and the eighth to score six times in a game. His six-goal total was one short of the all-time record of seven, held by Joe Malone of Quebec, a mark set in 1920. Half a dozen goals, plus four assists, added up to the greatest individual-scoring performance in NHL history.

Sittler not only set two league records and tied a third, he shattered four team marks. He also shattered the big-league dreams of young Dave Reece, for the Boston goalie was dispatched to the minors and never played another NHL game.

"The record-tying (sixth) goal was a lucky one," Sittler told reporters. "I tried a pass from behind the net and it hit Brad Park's skate and went in. But the thing I'll always remember about that game was the ovation I received when I broke the record with my ninth point. It was unbelievable."

Before the next home game, Sittler received an unexpected reward from Leaf owner Harold Ballard, a silver tea service worth several thousand dollars.

Fast Start, Fast Finish

NO PLAYER HAS EVER MADE as spectacular a debut in the NHL as Don Murdoch, the New York Rangers' number-one draft choice in 1976. Murdoch scored eight goals in the first three games, including five in one game, to tie a rookie record.

Halfway through his rookie season he had 32 goals. He was well on his way to a record number of goals by a rookie. Then ankle injuries kept him sidelined for several games, costing him the record and rookie-of-the-year honors. However, his fast start made him an instant celebrity in Manhattan. Ranger fans called him "Murder" Murdoch, and at the bars and discos people bought him drinks and offered him other temptations. It wasn't long before he became a kid with a drinking problem and, in time, a kid with a drug problem.

Later Murdoch would say, "I was in the limelight and my life was moving so fast I didn't even know where I was going. I fell in with the wrong crowd and that was a big mistake."

After Murdoch's second season, on his way home to Cranbrook, B.C., a small amount of cocaine was found in his suitcase by customs agents in Toronto. Murdoch was arrested and charged with possession. In court, he was given a suspended sentence and fined $400. But NHL President John Ziegler wanted to make an example of Murdoch, as a warning to other players to stay clear of drugs. He suspended the Ranger sniper for a year.

Eventually, Murdoch's case came up for review, and Ziegler lifted the suspension after 40 games. Ziegler said he hoped Murdoch had put his past difficulties behind him and that he would resume his career, one that showed so much promise.

Murdoch was delighted to get a second chance and couldn't wait to show his fans that his off-ice problems were behind him. But he never recaptured the form that had made him a rookie sensation and the toast of New York. After the Rangers cooled on him, he had stops in Detroit and Edmonton before drifting off to the minors.

Flight to Freedom

IT WAS AUGUST OF 1980. Two officials of the Quebec Nordiques, Marcel Aubut and Gilles Leger, were in Austria, ostensibly to scout hockey players in the European Cup Tournament. But during the tourney, a secret meeting was arranged between the two Quebecers and the famous Stastny brothers of Czechoslovakia, three of the best hockey players in the world.

What transpired at the meeting has never been fully disclosed, but it's certain the Czech stars were offered huge salaries if they would defect from their homeland and leave immediately for Canada. Marion Stastny, the oldest brother, decided against the move, but he urged his younger brothers to jump to the NHL. The following day, after the final game of the tournament, Peter and Anton Stastny mysteriously disappeared.

Aubut and Leger had arranged for the Stastnys, accompanied by Peter's pregnant wife, Darina, to be spirited to Vienna. The two hockey stars traveled in fear that the Czech secret police would overtake them and force them to return to Czechosloviakia, where they would face severe punishment.

From Vienna the Stastnys flew to Amsterdam, then on to Montreal, and finally to Quebec City.

When reporters asked Aubut if he'd landed the Czech stars at a bargain price because of their lack of knowledge of NHL contracts, he laughed and said, "No way. Someone in Montreal had been sending the boys the *Hockey News* every week. They knew all about the salary structure in the league."

The investment in the two brothers paid off handsomely for the Nordiques. Peter Stastny scored 109 points in his rookie season and won the Calder Trophy. Anton played well, too. The following year, in a dash to freedom almost as dramatic as that of his brothers, Marion joined the Nordiques and became an immediate star.

Goalie Hextall's Long-shot Goals

IN 1979 GOALTENDER BILLY SMITH of the Islanders received credit for scoring a goal against the Colorado Rockies, a "first" in the NHL. But Smith's goal was tainted. He didn't actually shoot the puck into the Colorado net that night. He was simply the last Islander to touch the puck before an opposing player accidentally scored on his own team.

But on December 8, 1987 in Philadelphia, goalie Ron Hextall did what no other goalie had done in 71 years of NHL play. With the Flyers leading Boston 4–2, and the Boston goalie on the bench with time running out, Gord Kluzak flipped the puck into the Flyer zone. Hextall stopped the disk and wristed it high in the air down the ice. It landed on the Bruin blue line and slid the rest of the way into the empty net.

Hextall, who can shoot the puck better than any goalie in history, took the achievement in stride. "I don't mean to sound cocky," he said, "but I knew I could do it. I knew it was just a matter of time before I flipped one in. It'll be something to talk about when I'm finished with hockey. And by then, maybe I'll have scored another one."

Just 122 games later, in a playoff series between Philadelphia and Washington, Hextall did score another — the first goal by a goalie in Stanley Cup history. With the Caps trailing 7–5 late in the third period, and the Washington goalie replaced by an extra shooter, Hextall trapped the puck behind his net, saw an opening and flipped it high in the air. The puck skipped once inside the Caps' blue line and skidded into the empty net. It was almost a carbon copy of his regular season goal.

Washington general manager David Poile, who witnessed the historic goal that helped send his team to defeat, told reporters after the game, "Bobby Orr, Wayne Gretzky, Mario Lemieux, they all changed the game. Now Hextall's changing it, too."

In the Flyers' dressing room, one of Hextall's teammates quipped, "Some of the teams will have to start shadowing him now."

Thumbs Up for Pat Verbeek

PAT VERBEEK OF THE HARTFORD WHALERS has been averaging more than 40 goals per season for the past four years and is regarded as one of the premier right-wingers in hockey. He's also one of the luckiest players in the game because his career had apparently ended suddenly several years ago.

While he was working on his 200-acre farm near Forest, Ont. in May 1985, Verbeek's left thumb was completely severed when he caught his hand in a corn-planting machine. The thumb dropped into a load of fertilizer and disappeared. While Pat was rushed to a nearby hospital in Sarnia, his parents searched frantically through the fertilizer. The thumb was finally located and brought to the operating room, where Dr. Brian Evans hastily reattached it. But he didn't offer much hope that the operation would be a success.

Verbeek was a member of the New Jersey Devils then, and the team thought they'd lost the services of one of their best young players. "I couldn't conceive of him coming back from such an injury," moaned general manager Max McNab. "Let's face it, a hockey player can't grip a stick without a healthy thumb."

By training camp, Verbeek was lifting weights and squeezing grips to strengthen his hand. And he told McNab and all the skeptics that he'd be ready to play when the regular season began. "I think the thumb has even grown a bit," Pat quipped at the time. "Probably because of that fertilizer it fell in."

He wasn't quite ready to play in the league opener against Philadelphia. But three games later he took a regular shift, told McNab the thumb felt "good as new" and went on to enjoy a 25-goal season. Since the injury he's scored 218 goals.

The Kid Could Always Score

WAYNE GRETZKY'S ACCOMPLISHMENTS as a professional hockey player are well documented and mind-boggling. But some of the records he set as a pint-size player in minor hockey are equally astonishing.

Wayne's first season of organized hockey was nothing special. In fact, as a five-year-old playing on a team of nine- and ten-year-olds, he scored just one goal for his Brantford, Ontario team. His father Walter, an amateur photographer, managed to snap a photo of his big moment. After the season, Wayne's coach told him not to worry, there'd be lots more goals to come. "You're just a little fellow but you've got lots of talent," he said. How right he was.

In his second season, Wayne scored 27 goals and in his third, 104. Then as a nine-year-old he scored 196 goals — plus 120 assists. No one in minor-hockey circles could recall a player ever being so prolific.

But Wayne had more surprises in store. By the time he reached peewee level, he was phenomenal. He scored 378 goals in 82 games, even though he was checked closely by opposing teams.

"And he wasn't a puck hog, either," states former teammate Greg Stefan, who went on to become an NHL goaltender. "He was always setting up his teammates with unbelievable plays."

The unbeaten Toronto Cedar Hill team played in Brantford one day and lost 6–0 when Gretzky scored four goals and added two assists. In a return match in Toronto, Cedar Hill was leading 8–0 when Gretzky sparked a miraculous comeback in the third period, leading his team to an 11–10 triumph.

In one tournament, he scored 50 goals in nine games, and by the time he was 13 he'd already scored the incredible total of 1000 goals. At the Quebec City Peewee Tournament one year, his dazzling play earned him the nickname White Tornado. He acquired two more nicknames in junior hockey — Ink for all the press attention he attracted and Pencil because he was so thin.

He even scored 158 goals one season in another sport — lacrosse!

At age 17, Wayne signed his first pro contract with the Indianapolis Racers of the WHA, after drawing up the contract himself in longhand. It was for four years and $875,000.

Even in minor hockey, Wayne had the right side of his hockey sweater tucked into his pants because his sweaters were always too big for him. He still keeps his sweater tucked in, but now it's become a habit or superstition. He even uses Velcro to make sure the sweater stays that way.

There Was Nobody Like Number Nine

BACK IN 1980 hockey's most famous player decided he couldn't play the game forever after all. So at the age of 52, Gordie Howe put away his skates and stick and said goodbye to the sport he loved.

It marked the end of a fabulous career. Howe is the only NHL player who remained a scoring threat well into his fifties. He's the only grandfather to play in the NHL, and he's the only player whose amazing career spanned 35 seasons and five decades.

In his time, Howe established an awesome list of records. He scored more than 1,000 goals, counting service in two pro leagues. He was the NHL's leading scorer and MVP six different times and an all-star 21 times. In the WHA, he was an all-star twice and MVP once.

Gordie's initial retirement from the game was in 1971, at the age of 43 and after a quarter of a century in a Detroit uniform. He took a front-office job with the Red Wings but was bored with the few assignments he was asked to handle.

Two years later, he was lured out of retirement by the Houston Aeros of the WHA. Not only for the money — he received a million dollars spread over four years, more than he had ever earned in the NHL — but because it gave him a chance to play on the same team with his sons Mark and Marty. It was a "first" for hockey, and it didn't take long for Gordie to prove he hadn't lost his touch. He scored 100 points in his comeback season and led Houston to the WHA championship. Later, he served as president of the Aeros and became hockey's only playing team president. Later still, when Mark's wife had a baby, he became pro hockey's only playing grandfather. During his stint in the WHA, Gordie added 218 WHA goals to his Hall of Fame totals.

Soviet fans watching the final four games of an eight-game Summit Series in 1974 were spellbound by Howe's performance in a losing cause. Gordie starred for Team Canada (WHA version) in the rough series. The Soviets said it was incredible that a man in his late forties could be such a huge factor in such a fast-paced international matchup.

At age 48, Howe kidded reporters by saying, "I'm going to play another year of two but my sons are going to retire." After four seasons in Houston, the Howes moved on to Hartford, and with the merger of the two leagues in 1979, Gordie found himself back in the NHL. He scored his final NHL goal (his 801st) in his final game against Detroit in 1980. He was 51 years old.

Incidentally, Gordie Howe was a hockey Hall of Famer long before his playing career was over, another hockey "first." He was inducted in 1972, a year after he retired from Detroit and a year *before* he returned with Houston.

Wayne Gretzky has surpassed Gordie Howe as hockey's greatest scorer, but no one, says Gretzky, can top number nine when it comes to durability. "To play so well and for so long is simply incredible," says Wayne. "No player will ever do the things in hockey that Gordie did."

PART

UNFORGETTABLE GAMES

Wacky Happenings in Winnipeg

IN 1902 THE WINNIPEG Victorias hockey team held the Stanley Cup, and the city of Winnipeg was tremendously excited about a forthcoming challenge from the Toronto Wellingtons. There was such a rush for admission to the first game in the best-of-three series that four men at the front of the line were almost crushed to death against the arena doors by the mob behind; when the gates opened the men were trampled underfoot. Pulled to safety by arena officials, the unconscious four were passed over the heads of the onrushing fans until fresh air revived them and they were able to take their places in line again, this time at the end of it.

Some fans traveled all the way from central Saskatchewan to see the games and estimated they spent two hundred dollars apiece on the junket — almost a year's salary for many Westerners in that era.

The series was highlighted by some most unusual occurrences.

Before each game, the Winnipeg players warmed up on the ice while wearing long gold dressing gowns over their uniforms. Midway through the first game a Newfoundland dog jumped on the ice, halting play and precipitating a merry chase. The dog's owner finally followed his pet onto the ice and dragged him off by the ears.

Then the puck, lifted high in the air in an early-day attempt at icing, became lodged in the rafters over the ice. The players gathered below and threw their sticks at the rafters until one of them knocked the disk free. He received a standing ovation and bowed to the crowd.

When a player was penalized by the referee, he was told to "sit on the fence." Because there was no penalty box, the player sat down on the low boards (in some arenas they were only a foot high) until the referee waved him back into the play.

In those early days of hockey, when the puck flew into the crowd, it was traditional for the fan catching it to throw it back on the ice. However, in one of the 1902 games, a Winnipeg fan caught the puck . . . and kept it! He didn't know it, but he was starting a now familiar hockey tradition. He also caused a long delay while officials searched for a second puck. There was another delay when Fred Scanlan of Winnipeg broke a skate. Play was halted until he was fitted with a new one.

It was during this series, won by Winnipeg, that the puck actually split in two during a game. A Toronto player named Chummy Hill trapped half the broken puck with his stick, fired it into the Winnipeg net . . . and the referee ruled it a goal. Winnipeg goalie Brown complained to the referee, stating he thought play should have stopped with the breaking of the puck and he was taken by surprise.

How did Toronto fans, in those days before radio and television, hear about the outcome of the Winnipeg games? In the offices of the Toronto *Globe*, a newspaperman awaited the bulletins wired in from the arena in Winnipeg. When he was given the final score, he rushed to the telephone and called the Toronto Street Railway Company. A man on duty there gave three blasts on the railway whistle, which signaled the Toronto defeat.

It's reported the railway whistle could be heard from one end of Toronto to the other.

The Ice Was Littered with Loot

EARLY IN THE CENTURY, many top hockey stars were lured to Northern Ontario by mining moguls who'd struck it rich in the area. Towns like Haileybury and Cobalt paid fabulous salaries — Art Ross once received $1000 to play two games in the Timiskaming Mines League. A game played in the Cobalt Arena ranks as one of the wildest on record.

In a previous game in Haileybury, Cobalt's bad man, Harry Smith, who had been imported from Ottawa at great expense, cut down so many Haileybury opponents that the police rushed to the arena and carted Smith off to jail. But Smith wasn't behind bars for long, and he got a hero's welcome when he showed up back in Cobalt for the return match.

Staggering sums were wagered on the outcome. One man bet $45,000 on Cobalt to win. Wealthy mining tycoon Noah Timmins figured Haileybury was the better team and wagered $50,000 on his hunch. His bet was quickly covered.

Timmins was counting heavily on the goaltending of stout Billy Nicholson, at 300 pounds, the world's largest netminder. When Nicholson took his place in goal, there were very few openings for a puck to go through.

But it didn't take Smith and his Cobalt mates long to find a few chinks in Nicholson's armor. They scored five quick goals against the mammoth

goalie. Surprised and delighted to find themselves so far in front, the Cobalt players settled back to play a checking game.

Haileybury kept fighting in the second half, and with Art Ross showing the way, the visitors struck back for five goals of their own to tie the score before the final buzzer. The teams would rest for a few minutes, then play overtime.

With his $50,000 bet on the line, Noah Timmins invaded the Haileybury dressing room and waved a thousand dollars in the air. "This is for the player who scores the winning goal," he promised. For highly motivated Horace Gaul, the bonus represented a season's play. When play resumed, Horace grabbed the puck, rushed up the ice, scored the game-winner and collected the cash.

After the contest, delirious Haileybury fans showered the ice with money — unbelievable amounts of money. Players caught the bills and dived after the coins. But goalie Nicholson was the smartest of them all. He dragged a big washtub onto the ice and started filling it with cash. Then he turned the tub over and sat on it — all 300 pounds of him — until the hubbub died down. Nobody was going to dislodge him from his new-found loot.

A Bloodbath in Montreal

IF YOU THINK there's too much violence in modern-day hockey you wouldn't have enjoyed reading the headlines in all the papers after a game played in Montreal on January 12, 1907.

The front page of the *Montreal Star* called for six months in jail for the combatants in the Ottawa-Montreal donnybrook that had taken place the night before. One headline writer called it "the worst exhibition of butchery ever seen on ice."

Montreal's Hod Stuart, who for some reason played with bare knees, emerged from the game looking as if he'd been in a train wreck. Stuart had been nailed over the head by a hockey stick, a two-hander delivered by Ottawa's Alf Smith. For several minutes Stuart had lain on the ice like a corpse.

In another confrontation, Ottawa's Baldy Spittal smashed his stick over Cec Blatchford's head and Blatchford was carried off unconscious. Then Harry Smith, Alf's brother, whacked Ernie Johnston in the face with his stick, and blood gushed from Johnston's broken nose.

The next day, when the referee proposed to league officials that the chief culprits in the brawl, Alf Smith and Baldy Spittal, be suspended for the rest of the season, the motion was quickly voted down. The Ottawa boys weren't that unruly, the officials opined. In the heat of the game, they simply used poor judgment. The league president, who favored a lengthy suspension, was outraged at the decision and turned in his resignation.

Montreal police, meanwhile, shocked by the acts of violence on the ice, decided to prosecute. When the Ottawa team returned to Montreal two weeks later, the Smith brothers and Spittal were promptly arrested, charged with assault and released on bail. At their trial, Alf Smith and Spittal were convicted, fined $20 apiece and told to stay out of trouble in future. The evidence against Harry Smith apparently was less conclusive for he was found not guilty.

The Curse of Muldoon

THE CHICAGO BLACK HAWKS joined the NHL in 1926, and under rookie coach Pete Muldoon, the Hawks finished third in their division. Most hockey men thought that Muldoon had done a commendable job with the talent available.

But the eccentric owner of the franchise, Major Frederic McLaughlin, disagreed. He's reported to have accosted Muldoon and told him the team should easily have finished on top of their division.

"Not in my opinion," snapped Muldoon.

"Well, your opinion doesn't matter much anymore," McLaughlin answered, "because you're fired. I'll get somebody else to coach my hockey team."

And he did, hiring Barney Stanley.

That might have been the end of the story, with Muldoon fading into hockey obscurity, But Jim Coleman, a Toronto sports columnist and prankster of some renown, decided the story of Muldoon's dismissal needed embellishment, a humorous twist — if only for the chuckle or two it might provide his readers.

Coleman was a drinking man in those days, and soon after the cork was pulled from the bottle his creative juices were flowing. At the typewriter he concocted an angry exchange between Muldoon and the Chicago owner.

"You fire me," Coleman had Muldoon threaten McLaughlin, "and I'll put an Irish curse on your team that will last forever. The Hawks will never finish first in the NHL."

Coleman's readers, aware of his fertile imagination, chuckled when his story saw print. Coleman himself thought his column, like Muldoon, would be forgotten in a matter of days. And in a way, it was.

But a decade went by, then a second and a third. In all that time the Hawks never finished atop the NHL standings. Somebody, somewhere, vaguely remembered why. They'd been cursed by a former coach, Pete Muldoon. And the curse was working.

A story appeared about the famous Muldoon curse as if it were fact, and as the Hawks continued to be denied a first-place finish year after year, other wrote about Muldoon's strange hex over the Hawks.

Finally, after 40 years, with Bobby Hull and Stan Mikita leading the way, the Black Hawks surged to a first-place NHL finish in 1966–67. Finishing last was never a problem. In the 40 years since Muldoon's heave-ho, they had managed to do that on 14 occasions.

Today, whenever jocks or journalists write or talk about the Curse of Muldoon, teetotaler Jim Coleman, in Vancouver, now well into his eighties, just smiles. He remembers the night he invented the yarn.

Suspended — For Life!

OVER THE YEARS, many players have been suspended from hockey for various lengths of time, but only three times in league history have players received lifetime suspensions.

Back in 1927, during a playoff game between Boston and Ottawa, Bill Coutu — often known as Couture — of the Boston Bruins assaulted referee Jerry Laflamme and knocked him down. Then the player turned on linesman Bill Bell and tackled him to the ice.

All of this took place right in front of League President Frank Calder, who sentenced Coutu to a lifetime suspension and fined him $100. Teammates and opponents alike breathed easier with Coutu gone from the game. The ten-year veteran had established himself as a mean-tempered individual who would deliver as many crushing bodychecks in team scrimmages as he did in the games.

Five years later, Coutu's suspension was lifted, but by then he was too old to return to the NHL.

Two other players banned from the game waited much longer than Coutu to be reinstated.

On March 9, 1947, NHL President Clarence Campbell sentenced Billy Taylor of the Rangers and Don Gallinger of the Bruins to lifetime suspensions after he discovered they were associating with gamblers and placing bets on NHL games. Gallinger admitted later that he bet up to $1,000 on the outcome of the games, but that only a handful of games were involved. Campbell stressed that no fix of any game was involved or even attempted.

All efforts to have the pair reinstated, even long after their playing days were over, were rebuffed by Campbell and the NHL owners. The suspensions were not lifted until 1970, when both players were middle-aged. Taylor returned to hockey as a coach and scout, Gallinger did not. Their penalties remain the two most severe ever levied by an NHL president.

This Game Was Never Finished

ON MARCH 14, 1933, Coach Tommy Gorman brought his Chicago Black Hawks into the Boston Garden for a battle with the Bruins.

The Hawks were leading 2–1 with just two seconds left on the clock when Boston's great defenceman Eddie Shore rushed up the ice, shot and tied the score. Shore's goal forced a ten-minute overtime period. In that era, teams played a full ten minutes of overtime, not sudden death like today.

When the overtime began, the Bruins' Marty Barry promptly scored to put Boston in front 3–2, but the goal was hotly disputed by the Hawks. Referee Bill Stewart, whose grandson Paul is a current NHL official, skated over to the Chicago bench to explain the call to a furious Tommy Gorman.

When he heard Stewart's explanation, Gorman suddenly exploded in rage. He grabbed the official and shook him. He yanked the referee's sweater over his head and began battering him with his fists. The enraged Stewart, struggling to emerge from under his sweater, soon started pushing back. At least two of his punches left their mark on Gorman's ruddy face. It was a dandy fight, the players all agreed later.

Stewart had had enough of Gorman's belligerence. He threw the Chicago coach out of the game, and when Gorman balked at leaving, Stewart called for the cops. "Throw this man out!" he thundered, pointing at Gorman, who was still hurling insults at the referee.

Two of Boston's finest invaded the Chicago bench and began to wrestle with Gorman. The bewildered Hawk players didn't know whether to help their coach or not. But when they saw him being dragged away, they took off in pursuit. The cops called for reserves and threatened the players with jail if they didn't back off. Suddenly the visiting team's bench was empty — no players, no coach.

But that didn't bother Stewart. He pulled out his watch and gave the Chicago players one minute to return. When they failed to appear, he ruled that Gorman and the Hawks had forfeited the match. The Bruins won the abbreviated game by 3–2. It's the only time an NHL game has ended in this manner.

Ironically, it was referee Stewart who, four years later, took over as coach of the Hawks and guided them to the Stanley Cup.

The Player in Green

WOULD YOU BELIEVE ME if I told you that a member of the Toronto Maple Leafs once played in an NIIL game while dressed in a green uniform?

It happened on March 17, 1934 — St. Patrick's Day — and the man in green was, of course, that irrepressible Irishman, defenceman King Clancy.

Clancy threw aside his traditional blue and white uniform that night and donned a green jersey with a large white shamrock stitched to the back. It was his night — King Clancy Night at the Gardens — and there's never been a night quite like it.

Before the game, a number of colorful floats were wheeled onto the ice surface. Out of a large potato popped several junior players. Leaf star Harold Cotton emerged from a mammoth top hat. George Hainsworth, the goalie, was hidden in a boot, while Red Horner, the Leaf tough guy, fought his way out of a huge boxing glove.

Then, with the arena lights dimmed, Clancy, the king of hockey, entered the arena riding a float in the shape of a throne. He was wearing royal robes and a silver crown. Clancy's pals, Charlie Conacher and Hap Day, helped him down from his throne, and when he turned to thank them they impishly hurled coal dust in his face.

After receiving a grandfather clock and a silver tea service as mementos of the occasion, Clancy, his face still black and his uniform green, went to work against the visiting Rangers.

But after one period, Ranger coach Lester Patrick had seen enough. He collared King and asked him to please change back to blue and white because his green shirt was too confusing to the Ranger players.

Hockey's First Telecast

MORE THAN HALF A CENTURY AGO, in the winter of 1940, a game played in New York's Madison Square Garden made history. When the Rangers hosted the Canadiens that night, hockey fans at home could catch the action for the very first time, on a miraculous new invention called television.

Not many fans, mind you, because television was in its infancy in 1940. There were only about 300 sets in all of New York City. Their screens were a mere seven inches wide. Incredibly, there was only one camera to follow the play. The announcer's name was Skip Waltz, although he preferred to use the name Bill Allen.

A dozen years later, during the 1952–53 season, the first hockey games were televised in Canada. The Montreal Canadiens presented their first televised game from the Forum on October 11, 1952, and the Leafs' TV debut took place three weeks later, on November 1.

Incredibly, the first producer of the Montreal hockey telecasts was the 24-year-old sports editor of an Ottawa newspaper. Gerald Renaud applied for the job and landed it, even though he had never seen television and had no idea how to produce a game on TV. He hastily read some library books on the subject, asked other CBC production people how things worked and eventually did a praiseworhty job.

But televised hockey was not welcomed with open arms by certain league owners and executives. Many of them feared the medium would dramatically hurt ticket sales. Leaf owner Conn Smythe, for example, charged a mere $100 per game for TV rights to Leaf games during *Hockey Night in Canada*'s initial season. He wanted to make certain televised hockey would be in his team's best interests before locking himself into a long-term contract. At the same time, NHL President Clarence Campbell took a jaundiced view of television, calling it "the greatest menace in the entertainment world."

Killer Dill's Comeuppance

DURING THE 1944–45 hockey season, Montreal's Rocket Richard was the most talked-about man in hockey. Although he was hampered by a sore knee. Richard was averaging a goal a game and fans were wondering how long he could keep up the pace. It was the season he would go on to score 50 goals in 50 games, a remarkable feat. Rival teams did everything in their power to keep him from reaching the 50-goal plateau.

One night in New York, the Rangers assigned tough guy Bob "Killer" Dill to stop Richard. Dill had quite a reputation. He was related to two famous prizefighters, and he had been banned from the American League because of his rough play. He was looking for trouble against Montreal, and when he taunted Richard, calling him a "cowardly frog," he got it.

Richard's fist shot out. He flattened Dill with one punch, which left the Killer a quivering mass on the ice. When Dill revived a few minutes later, he tried to salvage what was left of his tough-guy reputation. He challenged Richard a second time, this time while both players were in the penalty box. Richard unleashed a series of punches, one of which opened a large cut over Dill's eye. Dill had never been so badly beaten, or so humiliated, in his life.

Both players were given double majors, and when Richard came back to play, Dill wasn't around to hamper his style. He'd had quite enough. The Rocket rubbed it in a bit by scoring the game-tying goal, his 19th in 19 games.

After the game, Ranger coach Frank Boucher, asked to comment on the fisticuffs, said: "That crazy Richard had better learn to control his temper. He's liable to kill someone one of these days."

The Rocket's kayo of Killer Dill served as a warning to other bullies in the league to beware of the Rocket's hot temper. He would not be intimidated, and anyone foolish enough to think he could be stopped with racial slurs or a raised fist was likely to end up as Dill had — flat on his back.

Dill, meanwhile, happened to run into the Rocket as they left the arena after the game that night. Through his puffed lips, Dill smiled and told the Rocket he'd never been in such a one-sided battle. When the Rocket said, "Let's have dinner sometime," the Killer said he'd love to.

Was It Murder on Ice?

THE NHL IS celebrating its 75th anniversary, and in all that time the league has had only one fatality in a game. That occurred in 1968 when Bill Masterton of the Minnesota North Stars died after striking his head on the ice while playing against the California Seals.

But the death of star player Owen McCourt of the old Federal League in 1907 was no accident. In fact, throughout the country, it was called "murder on ice," and there were demands that the player causing the fatality be sent to jail for life.

Owen McCourt, who played for Cornwall, Ontario, was the leading scorer in the four-team Federal League, an ancestor of the NHL. During a game with the Ottawa Vics on March 6, 1907, McCourt became involved in a fight with Art Throop of Ottawa. Soon other players joined the scuffle, one being an Ottawa boy named Charlie Masson. During the battle, Masson smashed McCourt over the head with his hockey stick. Unconscious, McCourt was taken to hospital, blood streaming from his wound. Within a few hours he was dead.

Masson was immediately arrested and charged with the murder of Owen McCourt. At the trial in Cornwall a few weeks later, witnesses gave conflicting testimony. While some indicated it was Masson's vicious attack that led to McCourt's death, others said McCourt had been struck on the head by another player just before Masson's stick creased his skull.

Judge Magee told a packed courtroom he was unable to determine which blow was the cause of

73

McCourt's death — in fact, it could easily have been a combination of the two. As a result, he had no alternative but to acquit Charlie Masson of the murder charge.

The Ottawa team, distressed over the death of McCourt, cancelled all their remaining games, even though the league championship was within their grasp. One of the Ottawa players said, "I never want to see a hockey match again. The game in Cornwall was frightfully rough, and poor Charlie Masson kept telling us to play clean hockey or not at all. I firmly believe that if he struck McCourt at all, he did it in self-defence."

Goal of the Century

IF HOCKEY FANS were asked to pick the greatest goal ever scored they'd have no trouble coming up with an answer. It would be Paul Henderson's famous goal that sank the Soviets and won the Series of the Century back in September 1972.

It happened in Moscow in the deciding game of the incredibly exciting eight-game series between Team Canada and the Soviets. Henderson's goal was a fitting climax to the most fascinating series ever played.

What many people don't know about that goal is that Paul Henderson almost wasn't around to score it. He almost sat out the most important game of his life.

In the previous game, in which he also scored the game-winning goal, he had fallen heavily into the boards, striking his head. Fortunately, Henderson

was one of the few pros of the time who believed in wearing a helmet, and the helmet probably saved him from a concussion and a trip to the hospital. He was still feeling the effects of his injury before game eight, and the team doctor suggested he let somebody else take his place. But Henderson said no. There was no way he was going to miss what might be the most important game of his entire career.

It was a decision he would never regret. In the third period of the game, Team Canada fought back with three goals to tie the score at five. Then, in the final few seconds, Phil Esposito whirled and shot. Vladislav Tretiak, the Soviet goaltender, made the save, but the rebound came right to Henderson, who was all alone in front. Paul shot once. Another rebound. He shot again, and this time the puck slid past Tretiak into the net. Team Canada won the game and the series. No one who saw that final game or even listened to it on the radio will ever forget Paul Henderson's goal. It was the goal of the century.

Recently, I asked Tretiak about his feelings when the puck went in. He said, "I think the Lord himself gave that goal to Henderson. It was a beautiful goal and a great surprise. Seconds earlier, Paul had fallen down behind the net, and I didn't even notice him. Do I dream about that goal? I can say with a smile, 'I think about it every day of my life.'"

Pelted with Pucks

BACK IN 1972, Derek Sanderson was the most highly paid athlete in the world. He jumped from the Boston Bruins and signed a contract, worth a reported $2.65 million over five years, with the Philadelphia Blazers of the WHA.

Blazer fans — more than 5,000 of them clutching free pucks given out before the game — were anxious to see the Blazers perform in their home opener. But Sanderson, who'd been named team captain by coach John McKenzie, was injured in an exhibition game and unable to suit up for the contest.

Disappointed to begin with, the fans grew ugly when the Zamboni resurfacing the ice had a breakdown just before game time. It broke through the surface and was axle-deep in ice and slush. Arena officials deemed the playing surface in the refurbished Convention Center unsuitable for hockey. To make matters worse, hundred of fans arriving late for the game had left their cars parked at all angles in the arena parking lot, creating a massive tangle there.

There was no option — the game had to be postponed.

The team owner, Jim Cooper, asked Sanderson to accompany him on the ice and announce the cancellation to the crowd. When Cooper and Sanderson took the microphone and delivered the bad news, there was a chorus of boos and cat-calls. Then the souvenir pucks started raining down — hundreds of them. But just before he ran for his life, Sanderson couldn't resist giving the crowd a parting shot. "Folks, if you think you're mad now, wait'll you try to get your cars out of the parking lot. It's a real mess out there."

Then he took off, dodging a hundred more pucks that came flying out of the stands.

Strange Objects on the Ice

OVER THE YEARS, I've seen some weird objects hit the ice during hockey games, especially during the playoffs.

Some of them were human, like the male streaker who vaulted the boards at Maple Leaf Gardens one night and made a run for the Leaf bench. Another night, in Los Angeles, three curvaceous ladies pranced from goal line to goal line clad only in their birthday suits.

Coins, programs and rotten eggs seem to be the most common items hurled by disgruntled fans. At the Los Angeles Forum one night, a Kings' fan tossed a live chicken, dressed in a purple uniform, over the boards.

A Detroit playoff series simply wouldn't be complete without a squid or an octopus making its annual appearance. Former NHL referee Red Storey says, "There's nothing as ugly or as slimy as one of those things on the ice. I'd always order a linesman or an arena worker to clean up the mess. I never wanted to touch one of them myself."

In 1975 a playoff game in Buffalo between the Sabres and the Flyers was held up by a low-flying bat, another creature players and officials try hard to avoid. Finally, Sabre forward Jim Lorentz whacked it with his stick, drawing a mixture of cheers and jeers from the fans. In the next few days, "Batman" Lorentz was inundated with letters. Most of the writers were sympathetic to the plight of the bat, and some even called Lorentz "heartless" and a "murderer."

In Quebec City several years ago, three little pigs, squealing in fright and dismay, were turned loose on the ice surface.

At the Montreal Forum in an era when it was customary to protect good shoe leather in winter, fans celebrated a big goal by the Rocket, Boom Boom or Big Jean by throwing their toe rubbers on the ice. Former Chicago Black Hawk winger Dennis Hull likes to tell about the time his father took him aside before a big game at the Forum. Anticipating a fatherly pep talk, Dennis was surprised to hear his father say, "Son, when the Habs score tonight and the rubbers hit the ice, grab me a good pair, will you? Size ten."

One Hot Dog — To Go

RETIRED PRO GEORGE MORRISON recalls an embarrassing moment in his career when he toiled for the St. Louis Blues.

"I was never coach Scotty Bowman's favorite player," said Morrison, "and I was even less popular with him after a caper I pulled during a game at the Los Angeles Forum.

"We were on a long road trip, and I didn't get on the ice for two straight games. During the game in Los Angeles it looked like the same old story — I was told to suit up but not to count on getting much ice time.

"It was late in the game and I'd warmed the bench all evening. Suddenly I realized I was very hungry. Well, next to me at the end of the bench, I saw an usher eyeing my hockey stick. So I whispered to him, 'Pal, get me a hot dog, will you, and I'll give you my stick after the game.' The usher was back in a flash with the hot dog, and I was just sneaking my first bite (I waited until Scotty was looking the other way) when Bowman yelled at me, 'Morrison, get out there and kill that penalty!'

"What to do? As I leaped over the boards, I stuffed the hot dog down the cuff of my hockey glove. I didn't know what else to do with it. And wouldn't you know, seconds later, someone slammed into me in front of our net. Hit me so hard the hot dog popped free of my glove and flew up in the air. Out goalie made a stab at it and tried to knock it to one side while the other players ducked the flying relish and mustard.

"Fortunately, the whistle blew and a linesman moved in to clean up the mess. That's when Scotty Bowman yanked me off the ice. By then, he'd pretty much figured out what had happened and he was furious."

Morrison grinned. "It was a long time before he played me again."

Brother against Brother

ON MARCH 20, 1971 I was fortunate to witness a unique bit of hockey history at the Montreal Forum. I was hosting a *Hockey Night in Canada* game between the Canadiens and the Buffalo Sabres, and our telecast crew gave the contest a lot of extra hype because, for the first time in history, we anticipated that two brothers — both goaltenders — would be facing each other.

The brothers were Ken and Dave Dryden.

Then just before game time came disappointing news. The brother against brother matchup wouldn't happen after all. While Buffalo coach Punch Imlach announced that Dave Dryden would be his starting netminder in the game, Montreal coach Al MacNeil turned spoilsport and named Rogie Vachon as the Canadiens' starter. It didn't seem to bother MacNeil that he was depriving the fans of being witness to a history-making event. They showed their displeasure when the starting lineups were announced.

The possibility of the two Drydens facing each other became even more remote when Imlach changed his mind at the last minute and started goalie Joe Daley in the Sabres' net.

Then in the second period, Rogie Vachon went down with an injury. He was unable to stay in the game, and off the Montreal bench to replace him came the tall rookie, Ken Dryden. Now it was up to Imlach to make a move. Sure enough, he pulled Daley off the ice and sent Dave Dryden in to guard the Buffalo goal. The fans went wild.

Both brothers admitted later that they were very nervous as they stared at each other across 180 feet of ice. When he wrote his best-selling book *The Game* in 1983, Ken recalled that encounter. "I didn't enjoy that game very much," he wrote. "I had played only two previous NHL games, and seeing Dave in the other goal was a distraction I didn't want or need."

Dave was just as conscious of the unique situation. Obviously, he was distracted, too, because he fanned on the first shot he faced, a hummer off the stick of Jacques Lemaire from 70 feet out.

Montreal won the game 5–2, but those in attendance talked more about witnessing a hockey "first" than about the final outcome. At the siren, the two brothers skated to centre ice, smiled and shook hands. Both received a prolonged ovation.

Whenever Kate Warbled the Flyers Won

AT THE SPECTRUM IN PHILADELPHIA, somebody decided that the American national anthem was too hard to sing. So, one night before the game they played a recording of Kate Smith singing "God Bless America" instead.

The crowd booed the rendition, and they booed it the next time it was played and every time after that. The Flyers would have switched back to the regular anthem except for one important fact — the team always won whenever Kate sang. They were 8–0 with Kate warbling them to victory. By then, the fans had warmed to the idea of an over-the-hill singer bringing the Flyers good luck.

Then somebody got the bright idea of bringing Kate in "live" to sing "God Bless America" — right at centre ice in the Spectrum.

But Kate turned down the first request for a personal appearance. "Hockey fans don't want to hear an old lady sing," she said. "I'm 66 years old. They'll laugh me out of the building."

It was true that Kate was 30 years past her prime. Nevertheless, the Flyers offered her $5,000 if she'd appear, and promised her first-class treatment, so she finally agreed to go to Philadelphia.

She arrived secretly before a big game against Toronto. The red carpet was rolled out, then the organ. The voice of the announcer boomed out over the PA: "Now ladies and gentlemen, 'God Bless America." Then he paused for effect and added, "With Kate Smith!"

Kate stepped onto the ice and the crowd almost knocked the roof off the Spectrum with the ovation they gave her. And when she belted out the song, everybody in the place had goose bumps. The Flyers won that night and when Kate made a second appearance at the Spectrum (by then her record was something like 37-3-1) prior to the sixth game of the Philadelphia-Boston Stanley Cup series in 1974, she sparkled again. The Flyers won the game 1-0 and the cup, and Kate was credited with playing a big role in the triumph. It was one of the most memorable chapters in Philadelphia hockey history, combining the talents of a remarkable old woman with a bizarre hockey club known as the Broad Street Bullies.

When Francis Fought the Fans

EMILE FRANCIS was coaching the New York Rangers at Madison Square Garden one night, and his club was leading Detroit 2-1 late in the game. Then the Red Wings' Norm Ullman split the Ranger defence, went in on goal and scored to tie the game.

But the New York goal judge was slow to react and didn't flash the red light for several seconds. When it did light up so did Francis.

He left the Ranger bench and dashed to where the goal judge sat. He berated the astonished official and demanded to know why he'd been so slow to signal a goal. Was it because the puck didn't go in the net? Should the goal have been disallowed? He demanded an explanation.

That was when a fan intervened and told Francis to butt out. "Leave the poor guy alone," the fan bellowed. Then he came out of his seat and lunged at Francis. The Ranger coach, already seething with frustration, belted the man.

Two more fans jumped up, grabbed the diminutive coach and began beating him. One roundhouse punch caught Francis squarely in the face, cutting him for six stitches. In the scuffle, the coach's suit was ripped.

The Ranger players then came to their leader's aid. Several Rangers scooted down the ice and climbed over the protective glass at the end of the arena. Skates flashing and fists swinging, they jumped into the fray and rescued their coach. Their sudden attack sent dozens of fans scurrying for the exits.

Two days later Francis was told the fans he'd struggled with were suing him for a million dollars.

It took five years for the case to come to trial, and just as the jury was filing out to reach their verdict, one juror whispered "Good luck" to Francis.

"Mistrial," declared the judge when he heard the remark. Two more years went by, and this time the claimants were awarded $80,000 in damages by a new jury.

"The incredible thing is," says Francis, "when the verdict was finally in, the three jokers who punched me and sued me then came over and wanted my autograph."

Why Wait for the Opening Whistle?

IT HAPPENED in the spring of 1987, in the Stanley Cup playoffs, and it brought shame to the National Hockey League. It was a playoff "first," and it caused the start of the sixth game of the Montreal-Philadelphia series to be delayed 15 minutes.

What was it? It was an incredible ten-minute brawl between the Flyers and the Habs, and it happened *before the game even started.*

The brawl was sparked by a silly superstition, nothing more, nothing less. Some of the Montreal Canadiens, for some obscure reason, had developed a habit of shooting a puck into the opposing team's empty net at the end of the pregame warm-up. They did it when most of the players had left the ice. Few people noticed, and few people cared. It was just a silly superstition.

But this night, when Shayne Corson and Claude Lemieux slipped the puck into the Flyer net at the end of the warm-up period, out stormed Flyer tough guy Ed Hospodar. He was incensed that the Habs would invade the Flyer end of the rink — even in the warm-up — and he attacked Lemieux.

That did it. Players from both clubs jumped back on the ice and a major brawl ensued. Forum fans had never seen anything like it. The next day reporters called the brawl "disgusting," "appalling" and "shameful."

The two teams were fined more than $24,000 each, and Hospodar was suspended for the balance of the playoffs as the instigator of the ugly brawl. He explained his attack on Lemieux by saying, "If it was that important to him, then it was important to me. Everyone is looking for a little edge in the playoffs."

It was the low point of the playoffs, and all because of a ridiculous superstition.

PART

TEAMS OF FAME AND INFAMY

McGill Boys Organize Hockey

THE RECORDS SHOW that ice hockey has its origins in Europe. In France a crude form of hockey was called *hoquet*. In Ireland it was hurley and in Scotland it was called shinty or shinny on ice.

There's no doubt that British soldiers, posted to Canada in the 1800s, played games of hurley or shinny in places like Halifax and Kingston, for both claim to be hockey's birthplace. Kingston has long claimed that the British garrison stationed in that city played hockey on the ice in Kingston Harbour in 1855, while Maritime sports historians say games were played in Halifax even earlier. There's convincing evidence a form of hockey was played on Long Pond, in Windsor, Nova Scotia sometime before 1810. Montreal historians also make a claim concerning a game between the Dorchesters and the Uptown Club played there in 1837.

Most researchers agree that Montreal deserves to be recognized as the site of the first game played indoors. On March 3, 1875, a group of McGill students introduced what might legitimately be called "the first game of organized hockey played indoors." The game was organized by James Creighton, originally from Halifax and a graduate of Dalhousie University. Creighton, who was about to enroll at McGill for postgraduate studies, arranged for some Halifax friends to send a couple of dozen shinny sticks to Montreal. With the help of the eager McGill players, he drew up some rules and booked the Victoria rink for the big game.

Because the game was played on a rink surrounded by a low dasher, with an ice surface of 80 by 200 feet (outdoor games were played on much larger surfaces), Creighton decided to limit the number of players to nine per side. In outdoor shinny, any number could play, and games involving twenty to forty players were common.

For indoor play, the rubber lacrosse ball used for a puck was found to be unsuitable. It was either pared off on two sides to produce a flat rubber object that slid rather than bounced, or it was discarded and a flat, circular piece of wood was used instead.

Two poles or flags were planted in the ice to serve as a goal area. It's reported that two volunteers served as goalkeepers in this game, which may have been another hockey "first."

The first game, won by Creighton's team by a 2–1 score, ended on a sour note. In his book *Hockey's Captains, Colonels and Kings,* J.W. Fitsell, a noted Kingston hockey historian, states that "heads were bashed, benches smashed and lady spectators fled in confusion."

Later on, Creighton and the McGill students introduced colorful uniforms, team positions, more elaborate rules and referees to enforce them.

Others may argue, but Montreal's claim to be the site of the first organized hockey game played indoors appears to be pretty solid.

The End of a Streak

SHORTLY AFTER the turn of the century, the Ottawa Silver Seven reigned as Stanley Cup champions. By 1906 they had defended the cup through eight consecutive series and won them all. They had lost only three of 20 Stanley Cup games played.

In March 1906, the Silver Seven met the Montreal Wanderers in Montreal in the first game of a two-game, total-point series. The Wanderers stunned Ottawa, thought to be invincible, with a 9–1 trouncing in game one. Did this signal the end of the Ottawa dynasty?

Back on home ice for game two, the Ottawa club began an incredible comeback in the series. After Lester Patrick scored for Montreal to give the Montrealers a nine-goal lead, the Silver Seven went relentlessly on the attack. They poured shot after shot at the Montreal goal, and at halftime the score was Ottawa 3, Montreal 1.

In the second half, the Ottawa attack was even more intense. The Silver Seven scored six consecutive goals to tie the series at ten goals apiece. There was bedlam in the arena. Nobody could recall such a comeback, the visitors were reeling in their skates and victory for the pumped-up Ottawa club seemed assured. It would be a triumph hockey fans would speak of a hundred years hence.

But wait! Montreal's canny Lester Patrick called for time. He took his panicky teammates aside and gave them a little talk. He told them to stop playing defensive hockey, to fight back with some offensive rushes. He reminded them of the disgrace involved in losing after holding a 10–0 lead. The strategy worked. When play resumed, Montreal went straight to the attack. Patrick himself scored two quick goals and the Ottawa firepower was suddenly defused.

Montreal held on to win th series 12 goals to 10, and Ottawa's long reign as Stanley Cup champions was finally over.

The All-American Team

IN JANUARY 1937, Major Frederic McLaughlin, wealthy owner of the Chicago Black Hawks, made a startling announcement. He said he was very unhappy with his team's start (only one win in 12 starts by mid-December), and he was going to get rid of the Canadian players on his club and build a powerful team with American-born players.

"I'll rename my team the Chicago Yankees," he declared. "By this time next season there'll be only American-born players on the Chicago roster."

He already had four bona fide major-leaguers on his team, all of American birth. They were goalie Mike Karakas, defenceman Alex Levinsky and forwards Doc Romnes and Louis Trudel. All but Karakas, however, had learned their hockey in Canada.

Late in the season, with five games left to play and his Black Hawks destined for a last-place finish in their division, McLaughlin signed five more American-born minor-leaguers to NHL contracts, giving him a total of nine, or half the team's roster.

The newcomers were Ernie Klingbeil and Paul Schaeffer on defence, center Milt Brink and wingers Bun LaPrairie and Al Suomi.

In their first game, the two rookie defencemen were on the ice for all six Boston goals as the Bruins trounced the revamped Black Hawks 6–2. Manager Art Ross of the Bruins was happy to get the two points, but he protested bitterly to the league that McLaughlin's use of the American-born "amateurs" was farcical. "Not one of them had a single shot on goal," he griped.

McLaughlin stubbornly kept the new players in the lineup despite widespread criticism. His team won only one of the five remaining games, and the rookies looked particularly inept in a 9–4 loss to the New York Americans and a 6–1 loss to Boston.

Perhaps it was the outcome of those two games that convinced McLaughlin to abandon his dream. His Black Hawks never did become the Yankees of the NHL. But today, more than fifty years later, McLaughlin would have no difficulty finding enough American-born talent to ice a winning combination.

Looking for the Winning Edge

OVER THE YEARS, NHL teams have always looked for the winning edge; the ploy, the maneuver, the little gimmick that might bring success.

Back in 1960, the Detroit Red Wings tried something new — oxygen on their bench. Players gulped oxygen from the tank, hoping it would give them increased stamina and pay off in a goal or two. It didn't help Murray Oliver much. Perhaps that was because he forgot to turn the valve on the tank that released the oxygen.

The Red Wings once kept a container of yogurt in the dressing room. Players were expected to grab a spoonful of it every time they passed by. It, too, was supposed to improve performance.

The Rangers were also noted for off-ice gimmicks. One season coach Lester Patrick ordered his players to drink a glassful of hot water first thing every morning, whether they thought they needed it or not.

A famous restaurant owner in New York came around one time with a so-called magic elixir to sell, made from the secret recipe of Momma Leone. The elixir would put more speed into the feet of the sluggish Rangers, he promised. But after the team suffered a lengthy losing streak, the magic elixir went down the drain, along with the Rangers' playoff hopes.

Another time, a New York hypnotist, Dr. Tracey, was hired to hypnotize the Rangers into believing they were a winning team. The hypnotist knew his stuff. When he talked to the players, eyes soon shut and heads dropped to chests.

One of the Rangers, Tony Leswick, was so deep in a trance that coach Frank Boucher became worried. "They look so listless, so out of it," he complained. "And they've got a big game to play tonight." He ordered Dr. Tracey to snap his players out of their deep sleep.

They hypnotist said, "You're the boss," and in a few moments all the players were wide-awake.

As the players filed out for the warm-up, Tony Leswick winked at Boucher. "You gotta be weak-minded for that hypnosis stuff," he said. "The old doc didn't do anything for me."

Worst-Ever Season

CAN YOU NAME THE NHL team associated with hockey's worst-ever season? Would it be the Washington Capitals who joined the NHL in 1974–75 and managed to win a mere eight games in their initial season? Or the 1930–31 Philadelphia Quakers who won a mere four games in a 44-game schedule?

Neither of these lacklustre clubs can match a team of Chicago Black Hawks when it comes to ineptness on ice. In 1928–29, the Black Hawks set records for futility that may last forever.

That was the season the Hawks played eight straight games *without scoring a goal*. And in the course of that 44-game season the Hawks were blanked 13 more times for a total of 21 games — almost half the number they played — in which they failed to score even once.

The Black Hawks — called the Blank Hawks by some — averaged less than one score per game and wound up with 33 goals for the entire season. Vic Ripley, their most dangerous sniper, scored a third of the Chicago goals himself. He finished with 11 goals and 2 assists for a 13-point season. Can you believe it? Only 2 assists and he managed to lead his team in scoring.

Twice during the season the Black Hawks went an entire month without winning a game. They enjoyed a bountiful December, compiling four of their seven victories during that month.

Perhaps success went to their heads after victory number four, for they were shut out seven times in the next 14 games and failed to win a game in January. February was even worse when they scored just three goals all month. It was then they suffered through the incredible eight-game streak in which they failed to score even once.

It's appropriate that a player named Ripley figured prominently in the Black Hawks' long season of futility. For the story of their ineptness deserves to be chronicled in "Believe It or Not."

The Flyers' Famous Undefeated Streak

IN AMATEUR SPORTS there have been many impressive undefeated streaks. For example, in college basketball UCLA won 88 straight games many years ago, and the Oklahoma football team once won 47 in a row. But in all of the pro sports, the longest undefeated streak belongs to hockey — and the Philadelphia Flyers.

The streak the Flyers topped belonged to Montreal. In 1977–78 the Canadiens went 28 games without a loss, winning 23 and tying 5 before Boston spoiled their fun.

Just two seasons later, the Flyers took off on a streak that would soon draw the attention of everyone. After losing the second game of the season to Atlanta, the Flyers topped Toronto 4–3, and that was the beginning of a remarkable romp around the NHL.

Coach Pat Quinn deserves much of the credit for the streak. He changed the Philadelphia style that year, emphasizing speed and quick passes and eliminating much of the brawling that was a Flyers trademark in the early seventies. During the streak, the Flyers averaged only 17 minutes in penalties per game. When they were known as the Broad Street Bullies, some said they accumulated that much penalty time during the playing of the national anthem.

The Flyers were a little nervous in game 28 when they tied the Canadiens' record and even more uptight in game 29 when they broke the record with a win over the tough Boston Bruins. By then, hordes of reporters and television crews were following their every move.

In December they went beyond the mark of 33 games established by basketball's Los Angeles Lakers with a 5–3 win over the Rangers. As the new record-holders for pro sports teams, their next goal was to stretch their unblemished mark into the New Year. They did — but only for a week.

All good things must end, and the end came for the Flyers on January 7, 1978, in Minnesota. In game number 36, the Flyers were zapped 7–1 by the Minnesota North Stars, and hockey's most famous undefeated streak (25 wins and 10 ties) was finally over.

"It was great fun while it lasted," said Flyer captain Mel Bridgman. "We couldn't believe we went for so long without a loss."

Miracle on Main Street

NO ONE IN HOCKEY could have predicted that the 1980 Winter Olympic Games in Lake Placid, New York, would produce one of the greatest upsets in hockey history, a triumph so incredible it's often referred to as the Miracle on Main Street.

Main Street was the site of the Olympic Arena in Lake Placid. There, on February 22, 1980, Herb Brooks, coach of the U.S. Olympic team, gave his players a pep talk before their big game with the Soviet Union.

"You were born to be hockey players," said Brooks. "You were meant to be here. This is your moment."

Despite their unbeaten record in the tournament, nobody gave the Americans a chance against the Soviets. Hadn't the Soviets skated off with every Olympic gold medal in the past 20 years? Didn't everyone say they were invincible? Hadn't the young American team — average age 22 — been seeded only seventh before the Olympics began?

But on this day against the experienced Soviets, U.S. goalie Jim Craig was spectacular, far steadier than his more famous counterpart, Vladislav Tretiak. After the U.S. scored a pair of goals against Tretiak, he was replaced by Vladimir Myshkin. The Americans fell behind 3–2 in the second period, but they fought back to tie the score at 3–3 in the third on a Mark Johnston goal. Moments later, U.S. team captain Mike Eruzione slammed a screened 30-footer through the pads of Myshkin for what proved to be the winning goal. At the final buzzer, all of North America celebrated the thrilling victory.

It was a stunning upset. Mark Johnston, a two-goal scorer for the victors, kept repeating, "I can't believe we beat them. I can't believe we beat them. Now we're just 60 minutes away from the gold medal. I simply can't believe it."

And two days later, before millions watching worldwide on television, the young Americans captured the coveted gold medal by beating Finland 4–2 and completing the saga known as the Miracle on Main Street.

Following the Olympics, the gold-medal winners were flown to Washington where they were guests at the White House and where each team member was congratulated personally by President Jimmy Carter.

"Your victory was one of the most breathtaking upsets, not only in Olympic history but in the entire history of sports," the President told his guests.

The Homeless Hockey Team

COACH TOM WEBSTER knows all about adversity. An inner ear problem threatened to keep him out of the NHL coaching ranks when flying to games aggravated the condition. Because of the pain, loss of balance and dizzy spells, Webster was forced to resign as New York Ranger coach in 1986 after a mere 16 games. Months later, after surgery corrected the problem, he resurfaced in an enviable position as coach of the Los Angeles Kings.

No matter what he accomplishes at the NHL level, Webster will be hard-pressed to surpass an achievement that stands out on his minor-league record. In 1983-84 he took a team destined for the scrap heap and directed it to a championship nobody dreamed it was capable of winning.

Webster was coaching the Tulsa Oilers of the Central League that season. But he had major worries right from the start. The team ran into financial problems early in the year, and by mid-season the owners packed it in. They simply quit — but the players didn't. The players held a meeting and voted to struggle on — without any owners and without a home rink in which to play. League officials, understandably dubious about the future of the franchise, granted them permission to play out the schedule, with all their games to be played on the road.

Leaving wives and sweethearts behind in Tulsa, the Oilers stayed in cheap hotels and often slept on the team bus. They changed their name to the CHL Oilers but they might as well have been called

the Homeless Oilers. They were hockey nomads —
the only team in history without a home base.

Occasionally, the Oilers were able to practice in
Tulsa, on a rink located in a shopping mall. But they
skated without sticks or pucks because owners of
nearby stores feared broken windows and other
damage from flying disks. To stay in shape, the players moved a soccer ball around the ice. Webster
borrowed some tennis racquets and kept his goalies
jumping by whipping tennis balls at them.

Somehow, Webster's Oilers survived their season of grueling road trips, zero fan support and
infrequent pay cheques. Perhaps adversity tough-
ened them because they displayed amazing
strength in the playoffs, sweeping Indianapolis
aside in the final series to capture the league
championship and the Adams Cup.

"I'll never forget our victory parade," says
Webster, who was named Coach of the Year. "It
was held in the hotel bar. Then we marched outside and paraded around the team bus. The players on the team were very special. They accepted
every challenge and overcame every obstacle. I'll
always feel very, very close to them."

The Best-Ever Canada Cup

ALAN EAGLESON has often claimed that
the Canada Cup tournament features the
best hockey in the world. Millions of fans
who witnessed the finals of the 1987 event would
be quick to agree with him.

The '87 Canada Cup — featuring a three-game
final for the first time in history — produced

101

another classic confrontation between the best of the Soviets and the best players in the NHL. It also made teammates of two of hockey's greatest players, Wayne Gretzky and Mario Lemieux.

In the best-of-three final series, played in Hamilton, the Soviets took game one, 6–5. Then, in game two, Mario Lemieux scored three times as Team Canada won 6–5 in the second period of overtime.

The final game was simply one of the most exciting games ever played. Team Canada coach Mike Keenan played Gretzky and Lemieux on the same line in this crucial match — he'd placed them with other teammates throughout the rest of the tournament — and they clicked immediately. They were marvelous. Gretzky collected five assists, and Lemieux came through with his second straight hat trick — after Team Canada fell behind 3–0.

The goal everybody remembers was Lemieux's game winner. The score was tied 5–5 with time running out in the third period. He took a pass from Gretzky, who had carried it deep into the Soviet zone, and blasted a shot past goalie Sergei Mylnikov. It was Lemieux's eleventh goal of the series, a tournament record, and it came with 1.24 minutes remaining.

Team Canada held on to win the game 6–5 and the tournament, a tournament credited with making a complete player of Mario Lemieux. Prior to the Canada Cup, he had been labeled a floater by some hockey experts, notably Don Cherry.

In the Team Canada dressing room after the game, Mario said quietly, "I think I've answered a few questions about myself in this tournament."

A Costly Broken Curfew

IN THE CAMPBELL CONFERENCE finals of 1988, the Edmonton Oilers were leading the Detroit Red Wings three games to one. It would take a miraculous comeback for the Red Wings to advance along the playoff trial. One more loss and their season would be over.

Some of the Red Wings obviously gave up all hope of a comeback, for on the eve of game five, seven Red Wings went out partying. They stopped to have a few beers at a popular bar in Edmonton. And wouldn't you know it, they stayed far too late, broke curfew and were caught.

Well now, how much do you figure breaking curfew can cost a guy? A surprising amount, as it turned out. They were fined, of course — the maximum allowable fine of $500.

But that was just the beginning of their punishment. In the off season some of the curfew breakers were released or traded. That proved costly, because Detroit owner Mike Ilitch is known as one of hockey's most generous owners. When contracts are up for renewal in Detroit, most players leave the bargaining table feeling like lucky lottery winners.

Just ask coach Jacques Demers, who received a $50,000 raise from Ilitch that season, making him the highest-paid coach in hockey at around $300,000 per season. Or ask John Ogrodnick, who, when he scored 50 goals one season, received a $50,000 bonus from the owner, even though he was not compelled contractually to give one.

When the 1988 playoffs were over, and the league forwarded each Red Wing player $16,000 in bonus money, Ilitch generously matched that amount. So the Red Wings received an additional $16,000. All of them, that is, but the seven curfew breakers who stayed late at the bar.

So curfew-breaking proved to be costly for the seven Red Wings. A $500 fine added to the loss of the boss's bonus comes to $16,500. Too bad. That kind of money would have kept them in beer all summer long. Well, most of the summer, anyway.

PART

HOCKEY'S SUPPORTING CAST

Smythe's Folly

BACK IN 1927, a man named Conn Smythe bought a Toronto hockey team for $160,000. The team was called St. Patricks and the players wore green uniforms. They played in the old Arena Gardens in Toronto, which had a seating capacity for only 8,000 fans.

Smythe made many changes. He changed the team colors to blue and white, renamed the team the Maple Leafs, obtained some classy players, and soon he was turning fans away at the door.

That was when he decided to build a mammoth new arena for his team. But Smythe's timing was questionable. By then — the early thirties — the Great Depression was causing tough times, and people said the task was impossible. Some called the arena dream "Smythe's Folly."

But the skeptics didn't know Smythe. He and his assistant, Frank Selke, solved most of the problems. For example, the construction workers had to dig through 26 feet of quicksand before they could lay the footings for the building to be called Maple Leaf Gardens. Selke talked the workers into accepting shares in the company in lieu of cash. And just six months after construction began, the 12,000-seat arena was ready for the opening of the 1931–32 season.

On November 12, 1931, the new home of the Toronto Maple Leafs opened on schedule and fans filled the place. They saw the visiting Chicago Black Hawks beat the Leafs in the initial game, but the setback was temporary. Smythe fired coach Art Duncan and brought in Dick Irvin to assemble a winning combination. Irvin did a masterful job, and in the spring of 1932, the Leafs captured the Stanley Cup.

Smythe's vision was rewarded with a world championship and full houses for all home games. In fact, people came from all across Canada just to see the new home of the Leafs. "Smythe's folly" no longer was heard when fans talked of the modern ice palace.

Late in life, when Smythe was asked to name his best year in hockey, he said, "That's easy. It was the year we built the Gardens and then went on to win the Stanley Cup."

The Coach Answers the Call

IT HAPPENED IN MONTREAL during the Stanley Cup playoffs of 1928, in a final series between the Montreal Maroons and the New York Rangers.

After losing game one, the Rangers ran into grief in game two. Lorne Chabot, New York's steady goaltender, was felled by a Nels Stewart shot and left the ice with blood streaming from a cut over his eye.

Ranger coach Lester Patrick, with no spare goalie, asked permission to use Alex Connell of Ottawa, who was a spectator at the game. "No way," said the Maroons, aware that Connell had played six consecutive games for Ottawa earlier in the season without allowing a single goal. Patrick was handed an edict — either find a goalie in ten minutes or forfeit the game.

So white-haired Lester Patrick, age 44, who'd played in goal perhaps once in his long playing career, decided to put on the pads himself. He told his players, "You fellows check and check hard. I'll need all the help I can get."

If the Maroons felt that Patrick would be an easy mark when they saw him shuffle awkwardly onto the ice, they were mistaken. Patrick played remarkably well, allowing just one goal on 18 shots as the Rangers won in overtime.

After the game, Patrick was mobbed by his mates. In the dressing room, surrounded by reporters, he played down his remarkable feat. "I stopped only six or seven really hard shots," he said with a grin. "And my teammates saved the old man with their backchecking."

The Rangers, with Chabot back in harness, went on to win the Stanley Cup, and they were treated like heroes when they returned to New York. Especially Lester Patrick, the coach-turned-goaltender. Mayor Jimmy Walker, who'd recently hailed the return of Charles Lindbergh from France and organized a ticker-tape parade for Babe Ruth after his 60-home run season, embraced Patrick at City Hall while thousands cheered and flashbulbs popped.

A Race to the Wire for Clancy

IN 1930 THE OTTAWA SENATORS of the NHL found themselves in serious financial trouble. The Senators needed an infusion of cash, and the team's directors decided to sell their most colorful player, King Clancy, for the staggering sum of $35,000. Was any player worth that kind of money? That was the question other NHL operators had to ask themselves.

The Montreal Maroons expressed interest and so did the Toronto Maple Leafs. Leaf manager Conn Smythe wanted Clancy badly, but his team's directors refused to pay more than $25,000 for the little Irishman — even if he was regarded as one of the best players in the game. If Smythe wanted him badly enough, he'd have to find the extra $10,000 somewhere else.

Somewhere else turned out to be the racetrack. One of Smythe's horses, Rare Jewel, was entered in a big race. The filly was a nag, a real loser that Smythe had purchased for a mere $250. In a previous race, she'd finished dead last. Her trainer tried everything, including a flask of brandy, to stimulate her interest in racing. Even the jockey aboard Rare Jewel told his wife to put ten dollars on the nose of the favorite and to forget about Rare Jewel.

In the big race, Rare Jewel went off at 106 to one. But somehow she staggered home in front, paying $214. for a two-dollar wager.

Conn Smythe was the only one at the track that day who bet heavily on Rare Jewel. He walked away with close to $11,000. Smythe took $10,000 of the money and added it to the $25,000 agreed upon the Leaf directors and purchased Clancy. Later he said, "I paid a fortune for a heart, the gamest heart in pro hockey. Clancy also brought character, courage and devotion to the Toronto Maple Leafs." Smythe even sent Ottawa two fringe players as part of the deal — Art Smith and Eric Pettinger.

"With Clancy the Leafs have a chance for the Stanley Cup," said Smythe. And shortly after Clancy arrived, they won it.

The Ref's Last Game

THE OLD REDHEAD, Red Storey, once scored three touchdowns for the Toronto Argos in a Grey Cup game. He starred in lacrosse and hockey, too. But it was in the NHL, as a referee, that he became most famous, especially after a playoff game between Montreal and Chicago on April 4, 1959.

It was game six of an emotional semifinal series, and the score was tied 3–3 when Ed Litzenberger of the Hawks was tripped up by Marcel Bonin of Montreal. When Storey failed to call a penalty on Bonin the crowd screamed. They howled even louder when the Hawks' Golden Jet, Bobby Hull, went sprawling after a collision with Junior Langlois. Again, no penalty.

The partisan Chicago fans screamed at Storey. When play stopped, one irate Chicago supporter leaped onto the ice and chased after the referee, dousing him with beer. Storey grabbed the interloper while Doug Harvey, Montreal's all-star defenceman, rushed over and belted the fan a couple of times. Then another Chicago fan jumped over the boards and leaped on Storey's back. Storey flipped this fellow in the air and Harvey caressed him with his hockey stick on his way down.

The game was delayed for 35 minutes until order could be restored. After the Canadiens went on to win the game and eliminate the Black Hawks with a 5–4 victory, the shaken Storey said, "Now I know what it's like to have people coming at me, ready to tear me apart. There were 20,000 people screaming for my blood. They hated my guts. How can so many people hate so much?"

A couple of days later, Storey was in Boston, preparing to work another game, when he heard that NHL president Clarence Campbell had been highly critical of his work in the Chicago playoff game. Campbell told an Ottawa sports editor that Storey "froze" on the two penalty calls that so infuriated the Chicago fans.

That was it for Storey. Even though Campbell said his remarks to the reporter had been off the record, Storey's pride was deeply hurt. He turned in his resignation immediately and never went back to the game he loved.

After hockey, he turned to sports broadcasting and the banquet circuit, where he's always been in demand with his fascinating tales of days gone by.

The Original Two-Goalie System

IT'S QUITE COMMON FOR NHL teams to change goaltenders during a game, but at least once in Stanley Cup competition a team got away with employing two goaltenders at the same time. At the turn of the century, a wily coach of a team from Kenora (then known as Rat Portage) unveiled a unique strategy against a powerful Ottawa club in a Stanley Cup match. He benched one of his forwards and inserted a second goalie in his team's net. There was no rule against it at the time, and the coach thought two goalies would make scoring almost impossible.

OOPS!

He was wrong. The goalies stumbled into each other and left enough openings for the Ottawa boys to score. The strategy was quickly abandoned.

A rule was soon adopted preventing a repetition of the ploy.

Eddie Shore's Quirks

When Hall-of-Famer Eddie Shore bought the Springfield hockey club many years ago, he became notorious for running the franchise on a shoestring.

Don Cherry, who played under Shore, tells some fascinating yarns about Shore's idiosyncrasies. For example, until just before game time Shore could be found outside the arena parking cars. Then he'd dash inside, suit up and play for his team.

Some other economies: he told his players fifteen cents should be a maximum tip to a cabdriver, and soon no cabbie would pick up a Springfield hockey player. If a player had a bonus clause for scoring 30 goals, invariably Shore would bench him when the player drew close to his target.

Shore had many other bizarre ideas.

As coach of the Springfield club, Shore insisted his players practice tap dancing in hotel lobbies and ballet moves on the ice. He told one player he'd score more often if he combed his hair in a different style. He told another his legs were too far apart when he skated. So he tied the kid's legs together, then told him to skate. In practice, he sometimes tied his goalie to the crossbar, a lesson in how to remain standing upright. At least once Shore locked a referee in the officials' dressing room because he thought the man had done a poor job.

He prescribed his own special treatments and home remedies to sick or injured players. He told them he'd cured himself of cancer and that he'd survived eight heart attacks. He delighted in displaying his chiropractic skills — he'd had no training, of course — until bones cracked and body parts were properly aligned. "You'd ache for a week after he finished working on you," says Cherry. "Some players were terrified to get on that medical table."

Once Shore invited all the players' wives to the arena. They dressed for the occasion, thinking he'd planned a surprise party for the players. When the ladies arrived he sat them down and lectured them, telling them that "too much sex" was the reason for the team's poor play. "Be celibate," he ordered the wives, "at least until the playoffs are over."

He destroyed the NHL hopes of many players, who quit the game rather than play for him. Others credit his tutoring with making them stars. But it was never easy playing in Springfield, then known as the Siberia of hockey.

Once Shore traded for a player named Smith. When Smith walked into the Springfield dressing room, Shore said, "Where are your goal pads?" The puzzled Smith said, "But I'm not a goalie. I'm a forward." Leave it to Shore to trade for the wrong Smith.

Cherry says many players on other clubs had clauses inserted in their contracts, stating that under no circumstances could they be traded to Springfield.

The Eagle and Orr

AL EAGLESON hadn't really thought seriously about getting involved in hockey back in 1966. But that was before he met Doug Orr and his son Bobby.

The Boston Bruins owned the right to young Orr, but they weren't offering much to get his signature on a contract, a mere $7,500 for his first season as a pro, and $8,000 for year two.

Doug Orr was shocked at the offer — hadn't all the scouts predicted that his son was going to be an NHL superstar? So he approached Eagleson and asked him to negotiate with the Bruins on his son's behalf. Eagleson jumped at the opportunity, took a tough stance with the Bruins and wound up getting Orr four times the original Bruin offer.

Not long after that, Eagleson was asked to help players in Springfield of the American League. That franchise, under Eddie Shore, was hockey's purgatory, and the tales of Shore's shabby treatment of players were legendary. With the Springfield players about to mutiny, Eagleson stepped in and forced Shore to make some concessions. Peace was restored. Eagleson's reputation was made.

One day he was invited to join a secret meeting with some of the Bruins in Bobby Orr's hotel room. The players told Eagleson they were impressed with the work he'd done in Springfield. Could he help solve some of the problems players were having with owners in the NHL? Would he be willing to take the lead in forming a players' association or union?

Eagleson relished the challenge. He plunged right in, secretly getting commitments from players on every NHL team. On June 7, 1967, team owners were astonished when he gave them the bad news. From then on, under his direction, the NHL Players' Association would be a powerful force in hockey. And there wasn't a thing the owners could do about it.

Colleen Howe Steps In

FOR YEARS THE NHL refused to draft amateur players until they reached the age of 20. In the early seventies, that didn't seem right to Colleen Howe, wife of Gordie and mother of two talented teenagers, Mark and Marty.

"It's an asinine rule," she declared before the draft in 1973. "Say you had a son who played the piano. You put a lot of time and money into coaching him and sending him to top conservatories. Then, at 19, when he's ready for Carnegie Hall, they tell you he can't play there because he's not old enough. That's ridiculous."

Her words triggered a reaction from Bill Dineen, then coach of the Houston Aeros of the WHA and a good friend of the Howes. Everyone assumed the WHA, like the NHL, had a rule against signing players under the age of twenty. But no such rule existed and Dineen knew it.

Dineen created a huge stir at the WHA draft meetings in 1973 when he drafted Mark Howe from the Toronto Marlboros. Officials from other clubs shouted, "It's illegal. The kid's a teenager. He can't do that." Others scoffed at Dineen's selection and said, "Dineen just wasted a top draft choice. He's violated the agreement that exists between the pro hockey clubs and the Canadian Amateur Hockey Association."

Dineen replied, "Since Mark Howe is American-born, he's not governed by that edict."

To show how confident he was that the courts would back his decision, which they ultimately did, Dineen drafted Mark's brother, Marty, who was almost as good a prospect, in the 12th round.

The next day Gordie Howe received a phone call from NHL President Clarence Campbell. Campbell urged him not to let his boys sign with Houston, for it would be a devastating blow to the NHL. But Gordie said he couldn't deny his sons an opportunity to play professional hockey. The boys had worked toward that goal all their lives.

A few days later, Gordie had a suggestion for Dineen. If he was going to sign two Howes for

Houston, why not sign three? "Great idea," said Dineen. So Howe, at age 45 and after two years in retirement, fulfilled a lifelong dream of his own, by playing on the same hockey team as his sons.

Rebellious George Hayes

IN 1965, NHL LINESMAN George Hayes was fired by League President Clarence Campbell after a 19-year career in hockey. He had officiated in more than 1500 games, plus 149 playoff and 11 all-star games.

Sounds like Hall of Fame material, wouldn't you say?

But Hayes, who died in 1987 at age 67, always scoffed at the idea of a Hall of Fame berth. He maintained some of the capers he'd pulled upset too many people.

Once, for example, he threatened to throw the referee-in-chief off a moving train. Then there was the time he got in a fight in a restaurant, was hit over the head with a ketchup bottle and couldn't see for two weeks.

When the NHL instituted an insurance program for officials, Hayes was the only one who refused to contribute. The following season, he was irate when he discovered he'd signed a contract that contained an insurance clause. So he named his dog, Pete, as beneficiary.

Hayes's downfall came after he refused to take an eye test as ordered by Clarence Campbell. He told Campbell his eyes were perfect, that he tested them by reading the labels on the bottles in his favorite Montreal bar. That was when Campbell fired him for "gross insubordination." Hayes says, "Here they were worried about my eyes when their top referee at the time, Bill Chadwick, had only one eye."

But there were other transgressions. The NHL had a rule that game officials must travel first class on the trains and sleep in a berth. Hayes preferred to travel in the day coaches. He didn't mind sleeping sitting up, and he also saved the money he would have spent on first-class accommodation.

His dismissal by Campbell was the culmination of a long-standing feud between the burly linesman and the league president. Hayes said, "Campbell didn't speak to me for years except to give me hell. I never respected him much, either."

Nobody ever criticized Hayes for what he did on the ice. He was regarded as one of the finest linesmen ever to skate in the NHL. Hayes predicted his career would never be recognized by the league. He'd been too much of a rebel, he'd told too many people what he thought of them.

But big George was wrong. Less than a year after he passed away, the Hall of Fame selection committee voted him in. A little late, perhaps, but a popular choice. And how we'd have loved to hear his acceptance speech.

Downfall of an Agent

IN THE MID-SEVENTIES Dick Sorkin of Long Island was one of the most successful player agents in hockey. This former sportswriter with *Newsday* corralled many of the game's top stars, players like Bob Nystrom of the Islanders, Tom Lysiak of Atlanta and Lanny McDonald of the Leafs.

When McDonald turned pro, Sorkin negotiated a million-and-a-half-dollar deal with the Toronto Maple Leafs. He negotiated a similar contract for Lysiak, and in both cases the money was spread over five years. Needless to say, Sorkin's clients were happy with the services he provided. They predicted big things for him in the agency field.

Sorkin was one of the first agents to haunt the junior hockey playoffs and sign up young kids long before they were ready for the pros. He was a charming guy, and many young players were flattered when he showed an interest in them.

The players he signed had total confidence in him. In most cases, they allowed him to look after all their finances, a decision most of them would later regret. With each signed contract, and when the money started pouring in from the pro clubs, Sorkin maintained what was later called a "nickel and dime" accounting system. The players' confidence in his business procedures would have been badly shaken had they ever seen it.

In order to make more money for his clients — and for himself — Sorkin took the players' funds, and without consulting them, invested thousands of dollars in the stock market. When the market collapsed in the seventies, his losses were staggering — about half a million dollars. He began to panic — someday the players would ask for an accounting — and he sought an easy way to get the money back. In a matter of weeks he lost another $200,000 desperately gambling on sports events.

Finally, Lysiak, Nystrom and others became suspicious. They called for an investigation and Sorkin's reckless handling of their financial affairs was finally revealed. Most — if not all — of their money was gone. The agent was charged with fraud, found guilty and sentenced to three years in jail.

Sorkin served part of his sentence and when he got out he flourished again, but not in hockey. In his third career, he became a successful painting contractor in New York.

Bruins and Rangers Swap All Stars

WHEN DON CHERRY coached the Boston Bruins in the 1970s, three of his best players were Bobby Orr, Phil Esposito and Carol Vadnais. Cherry was particularly happy to have Esposito in his lineup because the big centreman had just turned down an offer from the WHA that would have paid him two and a half times as much as he was earning with the Bruins.

But the 1975–76 season began badly for Boston. With Orr out of the lineup with knee problems, the team stumbled from the gate.

In Vancouver in the middle of a long road trip, Cherry took a call one night from Bruin general manager Harry Sinden. "I've just traded Esposito and Vadnais to New York for Brad Park and Jean Ratelle," Cherry was told. It was a blockbuster of a trade, and Cherry was instructed not to tell anyone about it until morning.

At sunrise, Cherry hurried to Esposito's room and broke the news. Espo was in tears when he found out he was going to New York. "Grapes, I hate New York," he said. "I told Harry I wouldn't hold out for a no-trade clause in my contract if he'd promise never to send me there. We shook on it. Now look what's happened." As it turned out, Esposito discovered he loved New York. Later he said Sinden did him a big favor by sending him there.

Cherry moved on to Carol Vadnais's room. When told of the deal, Vadnais said calmly, "Harry can't do that to me, Don. I've got a no-trade clause in my contract."

Cherry was stunned. How could that be? He called Sinden and Sinden hastily looked up the contract. Sure enough, Vadnais could not be traded without his permission. But there was no way the two clubs could back out now; the deal must go through. Did the Bruins offer Vadnais a lot of cash to let them off the hook? No. The Rangers, who wanted him badly, came through with a bundle of money, and Vadnais was on his way.

The Innovative Roger Neilson

THEY CALLED ROGER NEILSON Captain Video when he first coached in the NHL because he was clever enough to introduce videotape to professional hockey. He was always on top of things, introducing new methods, looking for an edge.

When he coached junior hockey in Peterborough, Ontario, Neilson astonished the fans by replacing his goalie on penalty shots with a lanky defenceman named Ron Stackhouse. When the penalty shooter moved in, Stackhouse moved out and checked him — before he could get a shot away. It always seemed to work and finally the league revised its rules and banned the Neilson ploy.

When he pulled his goalie from the net late in a game, the goalie was instructed to break his goal stick and leave it in the crease. If an opposing player took a shot on goal, there was a good chance the puck would hit the broken stick and not go in the net. Again, the league was forced to revise its rules.

Neilson even looked to his dog, Jacques, for help on the ice. In practice sessions, Jacques would stand on the ice in front of the net. Behind the net, a defenceman would try to draw Jacques out of position by moving from side to side. When Jacques refused to go for the moves, Roger would day, "See, fellows, if old Jacques won't be fooled by fancy fakes, you shouldn't be either."

Neilson was equally inventive when he coached baseball teams in Peterborough. One day he substituted a peeled apple for a game ball in the middle of an important game. With the bases loaded and two men out, Roger went to the mound to talk to his battery. Unobtrusively, he slipped the apple into the pitcher's glove. Then he secretly gave the ball to his catcher.

When the opposing runner took a lead off third, the pitcher threw a wild pitch over third base. Peterborough fans groaned for it looked like a failed pickoff play. Smirking, the runner on third trotted home, only to be tagged out by the catcher, who'd been hiding the game ball in his glove. No wonder Neilson's reputation as a canny coach preceded him to the NHL.

Rolling in Dough

HE WAS A DOOR-TO-DOOR SALESMAN in the 1950s, selling pots and pans and struggling to make ends meet. But he had a dream — a dream of making pizzas and someday owning hundreds of pizza parlors across the land.

He saved enough money to open one tiny pizza store in 1959. Two years later, he opened another. Today, Mike Ilitch can point with pride to more than 3000 Little Caesar pizza store franchises across North America.

He was always a sports nut — he'd been an outstanding ball player in his youth — and with millions rolling in each year from pizza sales, he fulfilled another dream — that of owning a big-league franchise. He purchased the Detroit Red Wings from Bruce Norris in 1982 — a once-great NHL franchise that had fallen on hard times. Since then he's spent many millions trying to turn the Red Wings into Stanley Cup winners.

In the eighties, he spent a million alone on fading stars like Darryl Sittler, Tiger Williams and Ivan Boldirev. Warren Young, Harold Snepsts and Mike McEwen cost him another bundle of cash.

But his desire for college free agents cost him the most. A cool million for RPI's Adam Oates (later traded to St. Louis) and even more for Ray Staszak from Illinois-Chicago. When Staszak signed for five years at $1.4 million he became the most highly paid rookie in NHL history. It turned out to be a dreadful waste of money, because Staszak faded faster than a tan in Toledo.

...AND I THOUGHT MONEY COULD BUY ANYTHING!

Other Red Wings were well rewarded. John Ogrodnick was handed a $50,000 bonus when he scored his 50th goal one year, and Brad Park received a huge contract plus two pizza outlets for signing on with the Wings. Coach Jacques Demers became hockey's most highly paid mentor in Detroit.

Mike Ilitch is a generous owner. But he's learning a fact of hockey — big spenders seldom win Stanley Cups.

The First Goal Nets

WHAT WOULD HOCKEY be without goal nets? And yet, when goal nets were first introduced back in 1900, many critics said the game would be a lot better off without them.

Before goal nets were invented, two wooden poles stuck in the ice marked the goal area. And behind the goal stood a judge, handkerchief in hand, which he waved whenever the puck crossed the line.

Then some chaps substituted a pair of gas pipes for the wooden poles. The pipes were joined at the top by a curved metal crossbar over which some netting was draped. The idea was borrowed from the game of ice polo, which was popular at the time in places like Minnesota.

When the new goal nets were introduced in 1900, the *Montreal Gazette* said they helped turn an otherwise good goalkeeper into something resembling a wooden Indian outside a tobacco store. The poor goalie was practically nailed to his place, the paper stated. The possibility of his going in behind the goal area was reduced to a minimum, and if his skates got tangled in the netting, there was an excellent chance he'd break his neck. In short, he'd be worse off than an old Roman gladiator caught in the meshes.

The goal net was of no earthly use to the goal umpires, said the *Gazette*. The goal umpire couldn't possibly miss any goals unless he happened to be afflicted with some rare optical malfunction. There might be only one time in a hundred when the netting might be of use.

Meanwhile, the *Brooklyn Eagle* endorsed the nets and said they would revolutionize the game. They would eliminate frequent disputes, claimed the *Eagle,* and matches would then be won or lost on merit alone.

The American nets of the day differed from the Canadian model. American nets had posts made of rubber-covered iron pipes but fixed upon springs. When a player slammed into the post it bent right back to ice level, then sprang upright again.

126

With goalies nowadays griping about forwards who charge the net, without fear of personal injury because modern-day nets are easily dislodged, it's obvious that hockey still hasn't found the perfect goal net.

Playoff Fiasco in New Jersey

THERE WAS TENSION in the air before game four of the playoff series between New Jersey and Boston in 1988. Game three of the Wales Conference final had ended on a shocking note — with Devils' coach Jim Schoenfeld confronting referee Don Koharski in a hallway at the Brendan Byrne Arena. Schoenfeld was livid and called Koharski a "fat pig" among other things. For his outburst, Schoenfeld was suspended.

Between playoff games, in an unprecedented move, the Devils served the league with a restraining order from a New Jersey court, a directive that allowed Schoenfeld to continue coaching. NHL officials were shocked. They couldn't believe a member club would resort to the courts to plead its case. The repercussions were dramatic, and for a time threatened the completion of the series.

The New Jersey move triggered a wildcat strike by the game officials for game four, led by veteran referee Dave Newell, who demanded safer working conditions in the arena. In effect, the officials, including the backup crew, went on strike.

League officials frantically sought substitute officials and came up with 52-year-old amateur ref Paul McInnis, and two linesmen — 51-year-old Vin

Godleski and 50-year-old Jim Sullivan. Only McInnis could find a referee's shirt. The linesmen wore yellow practice jerseys and green pants and skated on borrowed skates. The combined age of the recruits — 153; their NHL experience — 0.

And where was NHL president John Ziegler while all this was going on? He'd disappeared and nobody could find him.

The game was played and New Jersey won. Later, peace was restored when the league agreed to rescind Schoenfeld's suspension until a hearing could be arranged. The NHL's regular officials quickly agreed to return to work.

Boston's Harry Sinden had the final word about the amateur officials. "We took three guys out of the stands," he said, "and the difference between them and our regular guys was marginal."

Lord Stanley Missed All the Excitement

WHO IS THE ONLY MAN named to the Hockey Hall of Fame who never played, coached, refereed, managed or owned a hockey club? He never broadcast a game or wrote about one in the papers. In fact, he never even witnessed a Stanley Cup championship game.

The answer? Why, Lord Stanley of Preston, of course, the man who as governor general of Canada donated the Stanley Cup to hockey in 1893. Shortly after that, Queen Victoria called him back to England, so he never witnessed any of the great contests for the trophy that bears his name.

PART

5

STANLEY CUP CAPERS

The Ref Went Home

IT WAS EARLY SPRING IN 1899. Eight thousand hockey fans filled the arena in Montreal for a two-game, total-goals Stanley Cup series with Winnipeg.

In game one, Winnipeg was leading by a goal with a minute to play. Then Montreal broke through to score twice in the final sixty seconds to win the game 2–1 and take a one-goal lead in the series.

Game two was equally close and just as thrilling. Late in the contest, with Montreal leading 3–2, Tony Gingras of Winnipeg was slashed across the legs by Bob McDougall of Montreal.

"Two minutes," said referee Jim Findlay, pointing at McDougall as Gingras, writhing in pain, was carried off to the Winnipeg dressing room.

"Not enough," screamed the Winnipeg players. "McDougall should be thrown out of the game for such a vicious slash."

When the referee refused to change his decision, the Winnipeg players berated him, then stomped off to their dressing room to cool off. Referee Findlay followed them into the room. When Gingras showed him the deep cut on his leg, he said, "All right, I admit I made a mistake but I'm not going to change my call now. And since you men don't like my refereeing style and you don't appear to be willing to resume play, I'm all through refereeing this game and I'm going home."

With that he got up and left. Took off his skates and went home. Officials from both teams were stunned. They chased after him in a sleigh and pleaded with him to come back. After all, this was no ordinary game. The Stanley Cup was at stake. Finally, Findlay agreed to return to the rink and complete his duties.

But by the time he returned it was too late. An hour or more had passed and most of the 8,000 fans had gone home. The Winnipeg players, some of whom still lingered in their dressing room, ignored Findlay's ultimatum — return to the ice within 15 minutes or forfeit the game. Some of the Winnipeg boys, it's said, had already dressed and started off on a pub crawl of old Montreal.

When the deadline expired, Findlay had little choice. He awarded the unfinished Stanley Cup series to Montreal.

The Strangest Cup Challenge

OF THE MANY CHALLENGES in Stanley Cup history, the 1904–5 season provided the most unusual. That was the season the famous Ottawa Silver Seven were challenged by a team from Dawson City in the Yukon, men who'd joined the Klondike gold rush a few years earlier.

The Dawson City Nuggets left the Yukon on December 19, 1904, and didn't arrive in Ottawa until mid-January 1905. Three of the players, including 17-year-old Albert Forrest, the youngest goalie ever to play in a Stanley Cup series, had started out on their bicycles. But the bikes broke down in the snow, and the three players were forced to walk 40 and 50 miles a day until they reached Whitehorse, where they were reunited with their teammates.

From Whitehorse, the Nuggets took the train to Skagway in Alaska, where they were stranded for two or three days. They travelled by steamship to Seattle, Washington, by train to Vancouver and then by another train across Canada to Ottawa. They were 23 days on the road, with no chance to practice.

When they finally reached Ottawa, without having skated in more than three weeks, they requested a postponement of the series. "Give us a day or two to get our skating legs back," they pleaded. "We haven't been on skates for almost a month."

"Sorry, boys," was the Ottawa reply. "We play tomorrow night."

The Dawson City players, stiff and sore from their long journey, lost the first game 9–2. In game two, Ottawa star One-Eyed Frank McGee went on a scoring spree that left the visitors reeling. McGee scored a record 14 goals in Ottawa's 23–2 thrashing of the Klondikers.

Despite the humiliating defeat, Albert Forrest, Dawson City's beleaguered teenage goaltender, was highly praised by Ottawa reporters covering the game. "Young Forrest was sensational," one of them wrote. "If it hadn't been for him, the score would have been double what it was."

Ice Hockey or Water Polo?

ARTIFICIAL ICE MADE its first appearance in Canada in 1911 when Lester and Frank Patrick had it installed in arenas in Vancouver and Victoria. Before its use became common, many Stanley Cup playoff games were decided on ice that was soft as butter.

In 1905, for example, when Rat Portage, now called Kenora, challenged Ottawa for the Stanley Cup, the Thistles zipped around the slow-footed Capital City boys to capture the first game of the series 9–3. The Rat Portage players wore new tube skates invented by a man named McCullough, and many credited the thin-bladed skates for their superior speed.

After game one, Ottawa fans resigned themselves to the loss of the Stanley Cup. Another win for the speedy Thistles in the best-of-three series and the trophy would go west.

But somebody in Ottawa — the canny (some say devious) perpetrator was never identified — came up with an ingenious plan to rob the visitors of what appeared to be certain victory.

When the Thistles showed up for game two and glanced out on the ice, their mouths dropped open in amazement. Someone had flooded the ice surface with two inches of water an hour earlier — even though it was well above freezing and there was no chance the water would freeze.

The Ottawa strategy worked. The thin-bladed tube skates worn by the Thistles cut deep into the soft ice while the layer of water on top nullified their superior passing and stickhandling skills. Ottawa, a more physical team, appeared to be quite at home in the water and slush, and tied the series with a 4–2 victory.

The screams of outrage from the visitors over the flooding of the ice forced the arena manager to produce a somewhat better ice surface for the deciding game. This greatly disappointed the Ottawa fans, who had enjoyed the swimming pool atmosphere of game two. Ottawa's Frank McGee scored the winning goal in a 5–4 triumph, and the westerners returned to Rat Portage, furious but empty-handed.

Their howls of protest echoed from one end of Ontario to the other. "Some sneak in Ottawa flooded the ice deliberately and it cost us the cup," they told one and all. Ah, but who could prove it?

Too Many Rings, Not Enough Fingers

TWO MEN SHARE the record of being on the most Stanley Cup winning teams. Henri Richard of Montreal played on 11 championship clubs. Toe Blake, also of Montreal, is the only other man to garner 11 Stanley Cup rings. He played on three championship teams and was the winning coach of eight other Cup-winning clubs.

The Cup Was Never Won

IN 1919, WHEN THE NATIONAL HOCKEY LEAGUE was only two years old, the Montreal Canadiens defeated Ottawa in a playoff series, then journeyed west to meet the Seattle Metropolitans, the champions of the Pacific Coast League, in a best-of-five series for the Stanley Cup.

In these days, "western rules" and "eastern rules" were in force in alternate playoff games, the major difference being that western teams used a seventh skater or "rover."

Under western rules, Seattle won the first game when the Canadiens had trouble making good use of their extra man. Under eastern rules, Montreal took the second game 4–2, with superstar Newsy Lalonde scoring all four goals. Seattle captured game three, and game four ended in a scoreless tie, despite 100 minutes of overtime.

Montreal evened the series by taking game five, but many of the players felt sick during the contest. Cully Wilson of Seattle fell to the ice complaining of dizziness and fatigue, and Montreal's Bad Joe Hall, also very ill, could not continue playing. He was rushed to hospital with a temperature of 105°F.

The so-called black flu epidemic was sweeping the continent in 1919, killing thousands of people, and several players on both teams were afflicted. At least five of the Canadiens found it impossible to skate and were confined to bed on the eve of the deciding game. Montreal manager George Kennedy, himself a flu victim, asked permission to use several players from Victoria as substitutes for his ailing stars, one of whom was Lalonde, who had already scored six goals against the Metropolitans. But Seattle refused to go along with the request. As a result, officials had no choice but to cancel the remaining game. It's the only time in NHL history a Stanley Cup series went undecided.

When the Canadiens staggered onto their train for the return trip to Montreal, they left Joe Hall, their popular teammate, behind. On April 5, he died of his illness in a Seattle hospital.

Clancy Did It All

IN MARCH 1923, the Ottawa Senators of the NHL traveled to the West Coast, where, after beating Vancouver in one Stanley Cup playoff series, they were challenged by Edmonton in another.

It was a two-game total-point series, and when Ottawa won the first game 2–1, the stage was set for a performance unmatched in professional hockey history.

In game two, when both the Senators' star defencemen were injured, off the bench came 19-year-old King Clancy to replace one, then the other. When Ottawa centreman Frank Nighbor went down, Clancy moved to centre ice. Later, Clancy played on right wing, subbing for the regular winger who had gone off to have a cut stitched up. After that, the versatile Clancy gave the left-winger a rest.

But Clancy's versatility was put to the ultimate test when the Ottawa goalie, Clint Benedict, drew a minor penalty. Off he went to the box, for in those days goalies were required to serve their own penalty time. Benedict casually handed Clancy his goal stick and said, "Here kid, take care of my net till I get back." For the next two minutes, Clancy bravely guarded the Ottawa goal and was not scored upon.

Years later he told me, "The story of my brief stint in goal was embellished by sportswriters later on. One of them described a number of spectacular saves I made. Another wrote that I not only made a remarkable stop of a breakaway but that I took the puck and raced up the ice with it, firing a hard shot at the Edmonton goaltender. It would be nice if these things were true but none of it happened. I didn't make a single save in those two minutes. Oh, I did fall on the puck once when it came close to my net, and Mickey Ion, the referee, said to me, 'Do that again, kid, and you're going off.' I said, 'Yes, sir, Mr. Ion.' "

Ottawa won the game, the series and the Stanley Cup, and Clancy made history. He was the only player in the NHL to play every position for his team in a Stanley Cup playoff game.

One Strike and You're Out

IN THE SPRING OF 1925, the Hamilton Tigers enjoyed the best record of any team in the NHL. As league champions, they drew a bye in the first round of the Stanley Cup playoffs and sat back to await the winners of the Toronto St. Pats–Montreal Canadiens series.

However, all was not happy in the Hamilton camp. Red Green, a star player, claimed that he and his teammates had played in six more regular season games than they had contracted for. He had a point, because the NHL had increased the schedule from 24 to 30 games, and many players hadn't been compensated accordingly. The sum the Hamilton boys had in mind did not seem excessive — only $200 per player.

When management said no, the entire team voted to go on strike. They vowed there'd be no playoff games involving Hamilton if their demands weren't met. NHL President Frank Calder angrily claimed the players' demands were outrageous, and slapped a suspension on the rebellious Tigers. "Your season is finished," he told them. Then he announced that Ottawa, as fourth-place finishers, would replace them.

That decision infuriated the other two playoff teams, Montreal and Toronto. "Why should Ottawa get the playoff bye?" they complained. "They finished behind us." Calder also drew criticism in the press, and ultimately announced that Ottawa would not participate in the playoffs after all, and that the winner of the Toronto-Montreal series would be the NHL's representative in the Stanley Cup finals.

The players' strike marked the end of NHL hockey in Hamilton. After the season, the franchise was sold to New York interests for $75,000, and the team was renamed the Americans. The striking Hamilton players were ordered to pay their fines and apologize to the league before being permitted to join the Americans for the following season. Calder did everything but give them a collective spanking and make them stand in a corner until they behaved.

Hamilton's only chance to win the Stanley Cup went by the boards in 1925 because of a squabble over a few hundred dollars. In 1991, the city of Hamilton was willing to pay millions for a second chance at NHL hockey.

A Tantrum Cost Him the Cup

IN THE SPRING OF 1942, the Detroit Red Wings were sure they were about to win the Stanley Cup, and so was everybody else. After a so-so regular season — a fifth place finish in a seven-team NHL and a record of 19–25–4 — the Wings were on fire in the playoffs. They polished off the Montreal Canadiens two games to one in one series and ousted Boston 2–0 in another.

In the final series against the Toronto Maple Leafs, the line of Don Grosso, Eddie Wares and Sid Abel was unstoppable. The Red Wings, with Grosso scoring twice, took game one 3–2. Grosso scored two more goals in game two and the Wings won it 4–2. They took a 3–0 lead in games over the Leafs with a 4–3 win in game three. One more victory and the Cup would be theirs.

But the Leafs fought back in game four after benching Gordie Drillon and Bucko McDonald and replacing them with Hank Goldup and rookie Gaye Stewart. Toronto was leading by a goal when a series of incidents set in motion a tidal wave that eventually submerged the Red Wings.

When referee Mel Harwood gave Detroit's Eddie Wares a penalty, for some reason the player picked up a hot water bottle from the bench and handed it to the ref. Moments later, a second Red

Wing penalty was called on Don Grosso. He dropped his stick and gloves in front of the referee and showered him with verbal abuse.

Toronto went on to win the game, but right after the match, Detroit coach Jack Adams was so incensed, he vaulted the boards and began pummeling referee Harwood with his fists. League President Frank Calder, who was at the game, subsequently suspended Adams until further notice, and he fined the two players, Wares and Grosso.

Without Adams to coach them, the Red Wings seemed to lose their confidence and most of their desire. The Leafs, paced by the Metz brothers, Syl Apps and Bob Goldham, rebounded to win three straight games and capture the Stanley Cup. No other team has ever accomplished such an amazing comeback in the Stanley Cup finals.

The Chicago Cup Caper

AFTER WINNING a record five straight Stanley Cups in the late 1950s, the marvelous Montreal Canadien streak came to an end in Chicago in the spring of 1961.

The final series between the Hawks and the Habs was an emotional one; Rocket Richard called it the dirtiest he'd ever witnessed. After game three, won by Chicago in the third overtime frame, Montreal coach Toe Blake's temper sizzled. He was so furious over an injury to Bernie Geoffrion and the officiating of Dalt McArthur that he chased after the referee and took a wild swing at him, a rash act that resulted in a $2000 fine.

Midway through game six, played in Chicago, Black Hawk goalie Glenn Hall was blanking the famous Montreal snipers for the second straight time. It was obvious to everyone that the Hawks were going to snatch the Cup away from the Habs.

In the crowd, shocked and angry, was a rabid Montreal fan. Ken Kilander couldn't stand the thought of a Chicago victory. But he was powerless to do anything about it. Or was he?

Impulsively, Kilander leaped from his seat and raced to the lobby of the Chicago Stadium where the Stanley Cup was on display, locked inside a glass showcase. He smashed open the showcase and scooped up the trophy, then ran out of the stadium into the night, with ushers and police in hot pursuit. The thief didn't get very far before he was apprehended and arrested.

In court the next morning he tried to explain his actions. "Your honor, I was simply taking the Cup back to Montreal where it belongs," he said.

"It doesn't belong there anymore," snapped the judge. "But you do. And you'd better get back there before I lock you up and throw away the key."

Graybeards Win the Cup

PRO HOCKEY in the 1990s is a young man's game. Most players are burned out — or nearly so — by age thirty. And yet not so many years ago, the Toronto Maple Leafs won the Stanley Cup with a whole team of graybeards; it was said they used rocking chairs in the dressing room and swigged Geritol from the water bottles.

When these geriatrics won their third and final Stanley Cup in 1967, the average age of the 20 players involved was a nice round 32 years. Three of them — Johnny Bower, Red Kelly and Allan Stanley — were in their forties, and eight more in their thirties.

Perhaps the most amazing player on the club was Bower. Determined to finish his career with Cleveland of the American League after kicking around the minors for 13 seasons (including a brief stint with the New York Rangers), Bower had been reluctant to join the Leafs. "I've had my day," he told Leaf management. "I probably can't help your club anyway." In time, he was persuaded to give the NHL one last fling.

Nobody knew for certain how old Bower was when he joined the Leafs in 1958 — he was at least 33 — and nobody seemed to care. For the next 12 years he supplied the Leafs with spectacular goaltending and led them to four Stanley Cups. But none was sweeter than the 1967 Cup victory over Montreal, when skeptics said the Leafs were far too old to be champions.

Old-timers they may have been, but most of the stars on that team — men like Bower, Stanley, Horton, Sawchuk, Moore, Armstrong, Keon, Mahovlich and Kelly — are now enshrined in the Hockey Hall of Fame.

Adventures of the Stanley Cup

SOME OF THE STORIES about the Stanley Cup and the men who've hungered after it border on the incredible.

You've heard, of course, about the Ottawa player at the turn of the century who drop-kicked the Stanley Cup into the Rideau Canal on a dare. The Cup was small then, just a football-size silver bowl, and fortunately the canal was frozen over.

Then there's the story of the Cup being left in a photographer's studio after he took a team picture, and when it went unclaimed, his wife used it as a flowerpot.

One spring, when the Cup could not be found, Harry Smith of Ottawa vaguely recalled tossing it into a closet in his home a few months earlier. Sure enough, a quick search of the closet produced the coveted silverware.

Then there's a tale from the twenties of a Stanley Cup celebration involving the Montreal Canadiens. The victorious Montrealers were en route to the home of team owner Leo Dandurand where a big victory party awaited them. In the back seat of their sedan, the Cup rested on the laps of the players.

Suddenly a flat tire halted the journey. While the tire was being changed, the Cup was deposited on the street corner. Repairs finished, the players jumped back into the car and sped off to the party.

With the victory celebration well under way, someone said, "Hey, where's the Cup we fought so hard to win?" Someone else remembered the flat tire and how the Cup had been placed on the curb.

Several players dashed for their cars and raced back through the streets until they came to the corner where the Cup had been placed. And there it was, waiting to be claimed.

Secrets of the Cup

THE STANLEY CUP is a handsome piece of silverware weighing about 37 pounds, and only the names of legitimate hockey champions are engraved on its shiny surface.

But such has not always been the case. For the Cup held high each spring by the proud captain of a celebrating team is not the original Stanley Cup. The original Cup — a small silver bowl about the size of a football — was passed from team to team for the first seven decades of its existence — ever since Lord Stanley of Preston, Canada's governor general, donated the trophy in 1893.

In the mid-sixties, NHL officials decided the original silver bowl was getting old and brittle, so League President Clarence Campbell quietly ordered a new one. Carl Pederson, an experienced Montreal silversmith, produced an exact duplicate of the original bowl and, when his facsimile was complete, he secretly substituted his creation for Lord Stanley's original gift. It was years before anyone outside the NHL was aware the switch had been made.

It has often been reported that only one woman's name has ever graced the Stanley Cup — Marguerite Norris, a former president of the Detroit Red Wings. Not so. Early in the century, Lily Murphy, a member of the Ottawa Social Club, scratched her name on the Stanley Cup — the first woman to do so.

And surely the youngest person to have his name inscribed on the Cup was Master Thomas Stanley Westwick, son of the famous player Rat Westwick, who starred for Ottawa shortly after the turn of the century. Young Westwick was just one year old at the time of the inscription.

Would you believe that at least two politicians have elbowed their way into the Cup-inscribing business as well? Of course you would. In Westwick's era, Dennis Murphy, a member of Parliament, and Sam Rosenthal, an Ottawa alderman, proudly scratched their names on the Stanley Cup during a victory celebration.

Lafleur Kidnaps the Cup

DID YOU KNOW THAT GUY LAFLEUR, one of hockey's greatest scorers, once kidnapped the Stanley Cup? It happened during a victory celebration after the Montreal Canadiens won the trophy in the spring of 1979.

The Canadiens were hockey's most successful team in the seventies and had just swept to their fourth consecutive Stanley Cup triumph, humiliating the New York Rangers in the final series four games to one.

After the traditional Stanley Cup parade through the streets of Montreal, and a further celebration in Henri Richard's tavern, Lafleur impulsively slipped the Stanley Cup into the trunk of his car. He then drove off to the home of his parents in Thurso, Quebec.

There he placed the gleaming trophy on the front lawn where friends and neighbors could see it and have their photos taken next to it. Word spread quickly, and it wasn't long before hockey fans from miles around, many of them clutching cameras, were hurrying to the Lafleur household. It's a day they still talk about in Thurso.

When the crowds began to thin out, Guy looked out the window to see his son Martin, garden hose in hand, filling the Stanley Cup with water. "That's enough," said Guy, rushing out to retrieve hockey's most important symbol. "The Cup is going back to Montreal right now, before something happens to it." And back it went.

While the residents of Thurso were enjoying Guy's little prank, the hockey men responsible for the Cup's safety, who had spent several anxious hours trying to track it down, were less amused. Guy was told never to repeat his stunt . . . or else.